THE WHIMBEY WRITING PROGRAM

How to Analyze, Organize, and Write Effectively

by
Arthur Whimbey
Elizabeth Lynn Blanton

Student Workbook

LEARNING Inc.
Mahwah, NJ

This Student Workbook is designed to be used in conjunction with the accompanying Instructor's Manual. Additional manuals and workbooks are available for purchase; contact Learning Inc., Sales Department, 10 Industrial Avenue, Mahwah, NJ 07430. Telephone 201-236-9500 or 800-9-BOOKS-9; FAX 201-236-0072; e-mail, orders@leahq.mhs.compuserve.com.

Copyright © 1995, LEARNING Inc.
All rights reserved
Printed in the United States of America
ISBN: 1-57004-030-3

Product design by Educational Publishing Consultants.

Table of Contents

	Page
Introduction for Students	vii
Text Reconstruction	vii
Copying from Memory	viii
Using the Writing Process	viii
Independent Study with This Program	ix

1. Creating Word Pictures 1
    - Section 1. Writing Directions for a Driver 2
    - Section 2. Description of a Buffet Table/Food Bar 6
    - Section 3. Holiday Cookies 9
    - Section 4. Thumbnail Description of a Woman 10
    - Section 5. Illustrating Personality Traits 12
    - Section 6. Description by Comparison 14
    - Section 7. The School Cafeteria 17
    - Section 8. Steel Drums from Striking Hands 22
    - Section 9. Analysis of Creating Word Pictures 26

2. The Writing Process 27
    - Section 1. Describe Things on a Wall 29
    - Section 2. Describe Yourself 31
    - Section 3. Where are You Now? 32
    - Section 4. Buy a Car or Furnish a Room 33
    - Section 5. What Do You Want to Do? 35

3. Describing a Sequence of Actions or Events 37
    - Section 1. Cause-Effect 38
        - Set 1. A Chain of Causes 38
        - Set 2. Multiple Causes 40
        - Set 3. Action with Both Bad and Good Effects 43
        - Set 4. "Sure, Dear" 44
        - Set 5. Smoking Dangers 46
    - Section 2. Describing a Process and Giving Instructions 48
        - Set 1. Describing a Process: Lawmaking 48
        - Set 2. Grandma's Cornbread 49
    - Section 3. Narrating a Series of Events 53
        - Set 1. Words Showing Sequence 53
        - Set 2. Vary Your Sentence Patterns 53
        - Set 3. The Practical "Un" Joker 55

	Page
Set 4. Smoking Addiction	56
Set 5. Biting Rage	58
Section 4. Analysis of Describing a Series of Events or Actions	62
Section 5. Independent Writing	63

4. Organizing Ideas into Patterns: Classification and General-Specific 69
    Section 1. Classification 69
    Section 2. General-Specific 73
    Section 3. Analysis of Organizing Ideas 77

5. Classification 79
    Section 1. Grades of Beef 80
    Section 2. My Car, the Image 82
    Section 3. Classification System for the U.S. Government 85
    Section 4. A Cheese for All Tastes 88
    Section 5. Not All Campers Camp 93
    Section 6. Analysis of Classification Papers 96
    Section 7. Independent Writing 98

6. Generalization Supported by Specific Details 105
    Section 1. You Can't Afford to be Sick 106
    Section 2. Pick Good Supporting Evidence 108
    Section 3. The Wonderful Plastic Card 109
    Section 4. The Family Needs a New Truck 113
    Section 5. The Perfect Pet 115
    Section 6. Ordering Supporting Details 121
    Section 7. Buyer Beware 124
    Section 8. Misplaced Convention Center 127
    Section 9. Analysis of Generalization-Specifics Papers 129

7. Beginning with a Thesis Statement 131
    Section 1. Two Parts of the Thesis Statement 132
    Section 2. Writing Your Thesis Statement 133
    Section 3. Presenting Specific Details for the Supporting Evidence 134
    Section 4. Taking Writing Competency Tests 136

8. Writing a Paper for a Competency Test: Brainstorming for Ideas 137
    Section 1. What Decisions Do People Make? 138
    Section 2. Brainstorming for Information and Opinions 140
    Section 3. Writing a Thesis Statement 143
    Section 4. Writing a Thesis Paragraph to Express a Mixed Opinion 146
    Section 5. Writing and Checking the Final Paper 148
    Section 6. Planning Your Exam Time 148
    Section 7. Other Competency-Test Papers 150

	Page

9. Comparing and Contrasting 151
   - Section 1. Comparison or Contrast? 153
   - Section 2. Comparison and Contrast Paragraph 154
   - Section 3. Point-by-Point Contrast Paper 156
   - Section 4. Block-by-Block Contrast Paper 159
   - Section 5. Chocolate Freaks Take Note 162
   - Section 6. McDonald's vs. Arby's 168
   - Section 7. Film or Print? 172
   - Section 8. Analysis of Comparison/Contrast Papers 178
   - Section 9. Independent Writing 180

10. Defining 185
    - Section 1. Football Fanatic 186
    - Section 2. Unwelcome Rain 188
    - Section 3. Physical Fitness 192
    - Section 4. Stepparent Blues 198
    - Section 5. Analysis of Extended Definition Papers 202
    - Section 6. Independent Writing 202

Next Steps: Analyze, Organize, and Write on Your Own 205

Introduction for Students

Most well-paying jobs today require a person to do a considerable amount of writing. Writing is also important in school and many other aspects of life. Unfortunately, many people find writing difficult. A major reason is that they have not learned the skills needed to write well. This program teaches those skills in a way that you will find interesting and effective.

Text Reconstruction

A powerful new technique called "text reconstruction" will make your study of writing skills stimulating and profitable. In text reconstruction, you are presented with model papers that have had the sentences within each paragraph jumbled. The jumbled sentences are like pieces of a puzzle that can be arranged into a complete picture. You read the sentences, analyze the ideas to see how each piece fits together with the other pieces, and arrange the sentences to form a coherent description or argument. Then, if possible, you compare your arrangement with a classmate's. If your arrangements differ, you each try to justify the arrangement you chose by explaining how you interpreted the sentences and the relationships among the sentences. You pinpoint the information in each sentence that made you decide to place it where you did among the others. Why did you put a certain sentence first? Why did you decide another sentence should follow it? What is its relationship to the previous sentence? How did you decide which should come next?

Arranging sentences and discussing different arrangements will teach you various patterns and strategies you can use for organizing ideas in your own papers. After you have completed a number of text reconstruction exercises, you will find it easier to write an effective opening paragraph to start a paper. You will also find it easier to follow that first paragraph with additional well-organized paragraphs to expand on your ideas. Just as studying the different moves of a star basketball player can improve your skill in basketball, studying the different ways paragraphs can be organized to communicate ideas improves your skill in writing.

Copying from Memory

In text reconstruction, after you arrange the sentences, you copy them in the arranged order. But don't just copy word for word. Copy from memory as much as possible. For each sentence, read as many words as you think you can remember and write those words from memory. Then check back to the original and correct any errors.

Copying from memory in this way is extremely powerful for improving all language skills. For example, teachers report that students who tend to make spelling errors improve greatly in spelling ability after using text reconstruction. Their spelling improves because, in copying from memory, they practice spelling words correctly. Copying from memory also improves grammar, vocabulary, and punctuation skills. One of America's greatest statesmen and earliest writers, Benjamin Franklin, used this method as a teenager for improving his language skills. Malcolm X also revealed in his autobiography that a program of copying models of good writing and then trying to recall the material from memory contributed to his powerful writing style.

Students who have used text reconstruction say they like it for several reasons. First, arranging the sentences into logical order is challenging. Second, discussing their arrangement with a classmate gives them an opportunity to express their ideas and to hear the views of others. And third, when they are asked to write an original paper, they have models to draw on for starting the paper, for organizing it, and for ending it with an effective concluding paragraph. Students also report that appropriate words and sentences come to mind more easily. Copying model papers provides a foundation of experience with language patterns and options. The verbal skills needed for academic writing become habitual and natural. Students find that their words flow more readily to form effective sentences and paragraphs, so they can express their ideas with greater ease, more powerful impact, and fewer errors.

Using the Writing Process

You will find learning to write with this program rewarding for still another reason. You will learn an extremely effective method for writing original papers—a method called "the writing process."

The writing process is explained more fully in Chapter 2. It is based on recent research showing that even experienced writers seldom just sit down and immediately write a perfect paper. Instead they go through a series of steps which help them find ideas, develop the ideas, and then express the ideas coherently in standard written English.

Your teacher may let you go through some steps of the writing process in small groups, discussing your ideas and early drafts of your papers. This is called the "peer response method" because you work together with your peers—your classmates. Here are some steps you may use in the peer response method.

1. Before starting to write, discuss the topic of the paper with one or several classmates to get ideas. You may take brief notes to remember key words and examples.
2. Write a first draft by yourself.

3. Exchange papers with another student and read each others' papers, or read your paper to a small group of classmates. They will tell you what they like about your paper—its strong points—and also where you might express thoughts more clearly or add examples to support ideas.

4. You respond in the same way to a classmate's paper. First discuss the paper's strengths: its interesting introduction, insightful observations, good examples, well-constructed sentences, and/or appropriate conclusion. Then point to any sections that you find unclear and make suggestions on how certain parts could be written more effectively or could use additional details.

5. Rewrite your paper based on any comments you found useful and any new ideas of your own.

6. Reread your entire paper to see whether it can be improved still further by adding more information or expressing points differently.

7. Proofread your paper for spelling and grammar errors. Reading a paper out loud often helps writers find such errors.

There is space in this Student Workbook for you to do most of the writing called for in the exercises. If you need more space, insert additional sheets in the workbook.

Independent Study with This Program

Although working with other students is enjoyable and beneficial, teachers have found that students who use this program alone, on the basis of independent or individualized study, also improve in writing ability. So if it is not convenient to work through the exercises with other students, you will find that going through the program alone is also profitable.

One final point: Many chapters have a section at the end with a heading like "Analysis of Classification Papers." Read these analyses carefully because they highlight major features of the writing patterns focused on in the chapters. In fact, many important features are not mentioned in the chapter introductions and are only in the analyses, where they can be illustrated with examples from the papers you have already reconstructed. Studying the analyses will teach you important concepts and techniques that you can use in your own writing.

You are about to embark on a program which has proven effective for strengthening writing skills—skills that can lead to higher grades in your other courses and a more prestigious, better-paying job when you leave school. Therefore, make a commitment to devote the time and mental energy required for the exercises and assignments to yield their maximum benefits. Your efforts will be well rewarded.

Chapter 1
Creating Word Pictures

Creating "word pictures" is a basic form of writing. How does something look? Where is it located? How does it sound, feel, or taste? Through a careful choice of words you can recreate for readers the sights and other sensory impressions you have experienced.

Being able to write vivid descriptions is an important skill for writing the various types of papers covered in later chapters. For example, in Chapter 5, different types of cheeses are described in terms of how they look, taste, and smell. Similarly, when you are comparing two things (Chapter 9) or arguing a position (Chapters 7 and 8), you must be able to describe people, objects, and situations to make your ideas clear and concrete.

The key to writing a strong description is taking the time to include plenty of details so your reader gets a full picture of the person or situation you are describing. Instead of just writing, "The man was smoking," you can fuel your reader's imagination with additional details like, "The man was puffing nervously on a long, thin cigarette." Don't just write, "The car drove very fast down the street." Tell the reader how fast: "The car sped down the street at over 80 mph." Here are some other examples:

Vague		_Detailed_
a high salary	~	$75,000 a year
a child	~	a three-year-old girl
a big car	~	a Lincoln Town Car
a very hot day	~	over 100 degrees
a big man	~	6'5" and 280 lbs

Such details are vital to good writing; they mark the difference between merely listing and vividly describing, between simply cataloging and dramatically recreating. These specifics help a reader visualize the impressions you are trying to communicate. Use the following exercises to sharpen your skill in writing descriptions of people and situations.

Many of the following sections ask you to write sentences in the best logical order. To obtain the greatest benefit, do not copy the words letter-by-letter. Instead, use these steps for each sentence:

1. Read as many words as you believe you can write correctly from memory (usually five to ten words).

2. Write those words from memory, including all capitalization and punctuation marks.

3. Check back to the original sentence and correct any errors you made.

4. Read the next group of words and repeat the above steps.

Generally you will be able to read, memorize, and correctly write between five and ten words. Sometimes you may be able to remember an entire simple sentence correctly. But with a large, difficult-to-spell word, you may only try to write that one word correctly from memory. Writing from memory will make you more aware of the spelling, grammar, punctuation, and word patterns used in standard written English.

Section 1
Writing Directions for a Driver

Exercises

Instructions. If friends are coming to a party at your home or are meeting you downtown to see a movie, you might have to write driving directions. This is one of the simplest forms of description, but your directions must be clear so the drivers won't get lost.

Exercise 1 (approximately 5 minutes). The sentences on page 3 refer to the map. Number the sentences so they are arranged into directions for getting from the corner of Adams and Oak to the movie theater on Central.

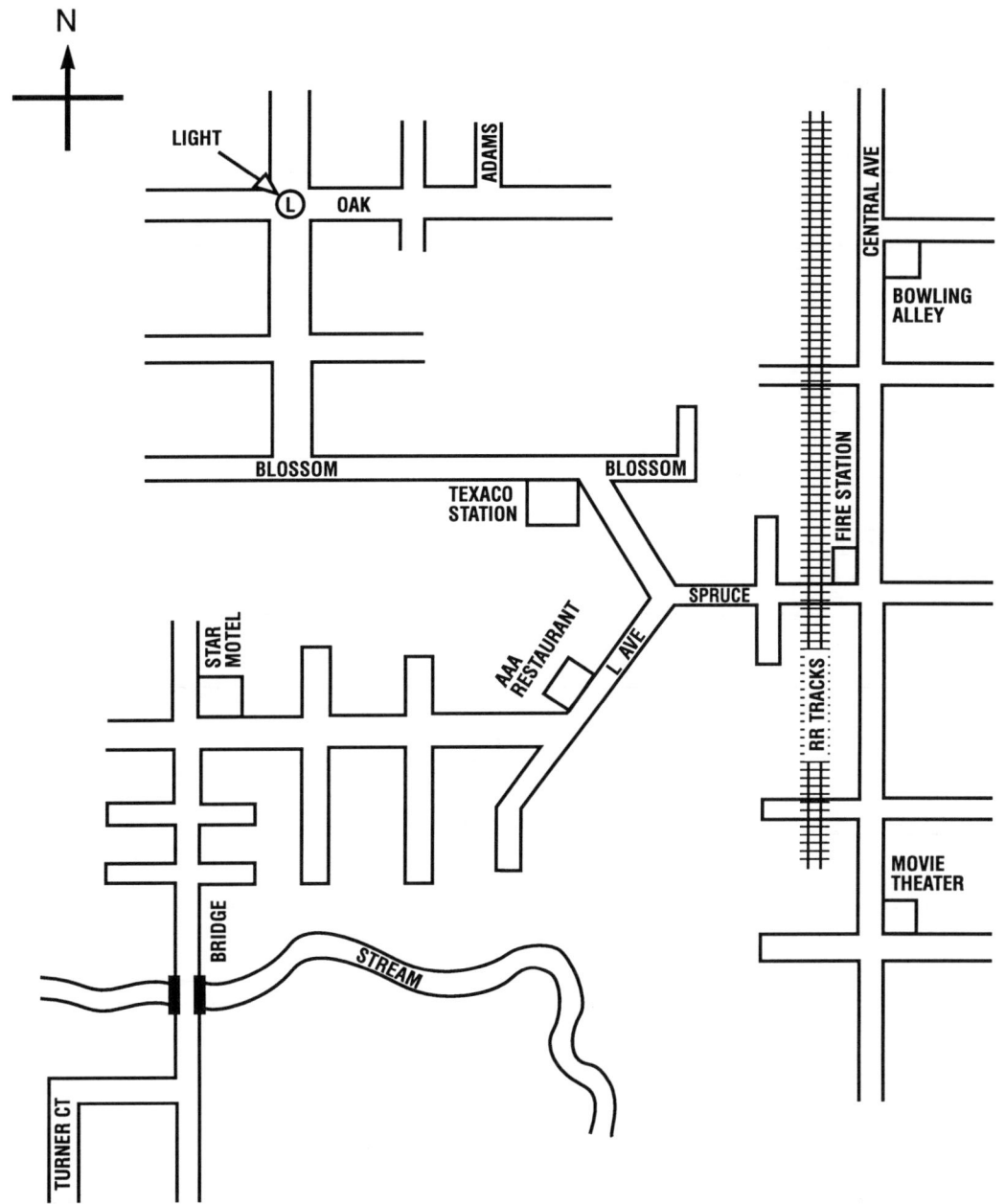

___ Go two blocks, which will bring you to the end of the road, and make a left onto Blossom.

___ You will come to a fork in the road, where you should take the left branch, putting you on Spruce.

___ When you get to the Texaco station, bear right onto L Avenue.

___ Drive for two blocks and you will see the movie theater.

___ Drive west along Oak Street to the first light and then make a left.

___ Go straight until you pass over the railroad tracks, and then make a right at the next corner.

Exercise 2 (approximately 5 minutes). Write the sentences in the order you numbered them to form directions for getting from the corner of Adams and Oak to the movie theater.

_____

_____

_____

_____

_____

_____

_____

_____

_____

_____

_____

_____

Exercise 3 (approximately 10 minutes). A friend wants to drive from the bowling alley to Turner Court at night, when it will be hard to read street signs. Write directions using easy-to-see landmarks: fire station, fork in the road, AAA Restaurant, Star Motel, and bridge over stream. Remember to mention in which direction your friend should start driving along Central Avenue.

_____

_____

_____

_____

Section 2
Description of a Buffet Table/Food Bar

Exercises

Instructions. The following sentences can be arranged into an orderly description of the buffet table/food bar depicted on page 7.

Exercise 1 (approximately 5 minutes). Number the sentences so they systematically describe the buffet table/food bar, starting with the table's location and then moving from the right end to the left.

____ Next to these plates is the salad section.

____ Moving past the salad dressings, you come to two pans of potatoes: mashed in back and French-fried in front.

____ The buffet table is against the wall, so you can only serve yourself from the front.

____ There is a large tub of shredded lettuce toward the back of the table, and in front there are four bowls with salad toppings: tomato wedges, cucumber slices, chopped green olives, and shredded cheese.

____ As you face the table, a stack of dinner plates and another stack of salad bowls are located at the right end.

____ Finally, at the left end of the table, there is a pile of napkins and a box with silverware.

____ To the left of the tomatoes and olives are three metal containers with salad dressings: French closest to the wall, Ranch in the middle, and Italian nearest the front.

____ Next to the mashed potatoes is a pan of gravy, in front of this is a pan of peas, and closest to the front is a pan of corn.

____ This brings you to the desserts.

____ To the left of these vegetables are three large meat trays, with roast beef in the back, fried chicken in front, and ham between them.

____ There is a large bowl of butterscotch pudding toward the back of the table, a platter of chocolate cake slices in the middle, and a stack of dessert dishes in front.

WALL

Exercise 2 (approximately 5 minutes). Write the sentences in the order you numbered them to form a systematic description of the buffet table/food bar from right to left.

The Whimbey Writing Program - Student Workbook 7

Exercise 3 (OPTIONAL, approximately 10 minutes). Cover up your numbered and written sentences on the buffet table/food bar and write a systematic description of the table, starting with its location and then following the path of a person moving from left to right—note this is the opposite direction to that in Exercises 1 and 2.

Section 3
Holiday Cookies

In the last two sections you described the locations of things. Now you will begin describing the "things" themselves.

Exercises

Instructions. For holidays, bakeries sell special cookies in shapes and colors fitting the occasion. In December, green cookies shaped like Christmas trees, with pink candy sprinkles for lights might be displayed in the bakery window. Writing descriptions of such cookies is the topic of these exercises.

Exercise 1 (approximatley 5 minutes). Write a sentence each for Halloween and Valentine's Day, describing the type of cookie a bakery might display. Let your sentences have this form:

For _____, _____ cookies shaped like _____, with _____ candy sprinkles
      holiday   *color*   *object*   *color*

for _____, are displayed in bakery windows.
     details on object

    Here are two examples:

- For <u>Christmas</u>, <u>green</u> cookies shaped like <u>Christmas trees</u>, with <u>silver</u> candy sprinkles for <u>lights</u>, are displayed in bakery windows.
- For <u>Christmas</u>, <u>red</u> cookies shaped like <u>Santa Claus</u>, with <u>white and black</u> candy sprinkles for <u>the beard, facial features, buttons, and belt</u>, are displayed in bakery windows.

    Note that two candy colors, black and white, are used to paint details on Santa. Use as many colors as appropriate to describe cookies for the following holidays:

Halloween: _____

_____

_____

Valentine's Day: _____

_____

_____

Exercise 2 (approximately 5 minutes). Here is a different description of a holiday cookie:

- At <u>Halloween</u>, bakeries sell <u>orange, pumpkin-shaped</u> cookies having <u>facial features</u> drawn with <u>yellow frosting</u>.

Write a description of an Easter cookie in a form similar to this.

Easter: _____

_____

Exercise 3 (approximately 10 minutes). Write descriptions of cookies for any two other holidays (e.g., Thanksgiving, Fourth of July, Mother's Day) using any sentence forms you prefer.

Cookie description: _____

_____

Cookie description: _____

_____

Section 4
Thumbnail Description of a Woman

Exercises

Instructions. These exercises deal with describing a woman.

Exercise 1 (approximately 2 minutes). Number the sentences to describe a woman in the following order: overall body (size, type), face, grooming (hair, clothes), and general impression.

___ Her hair was fashionably cut, and her clothes had been carefully chosen in a fine store.

___ She had high cheekbones, a strong jaw, and brown eyes that seemed to glow with vitality.

___ She was the picture of confidence and success.

___ The young, new manager was tall and trim.

Exercise 2 (approximately 3 minutes). Write the sentences in the order you numbered them to describe the person in terms of overall body type, face, grooming, and general impression.

_____

_____

_____

_____

_____

_____

Exercise 3 (approximately 5 minutes). Write a brief description of a friend or relative in terms of body type, face, grooming, general impression, and any other characteristics you consider important.

_____

_____

_____

_____

_____

_____

_____

_____

_____

_____

Section 5
Illustrating Personality Traits

Exercises

Instructions. When you describe a person with general words like "cheerful" or "ambitious," you can help your reader better understand what you mean by also describing some actions of the person that show cheerfulness or ambition. This exercise presents brief descriptions of actions illustrating personality traits.

Exercise 1 (approximately 10 minutes). Below are five sentences stating that a person has a certain personality trait. These are followed on the next page by five descriptions of actions illustrating the personality traits. Decide which description fits each personality trait, and then copy each description by the trait it illustrates.

Kathleen is ambitious. She _____

Paula is cheerful. She _____

Gwen has a good sense of humor. She _____

Linda is a considerate roommate. She _____

12 Creating Word Pictures

Louise is devoted to her children. She _____

_____

_____

- enjoys hearing new jokes. She often makes her friends laugh by imitating someone they know or by seeing the funny side of a situation.

- always says something friendly when you meet her. She doesn't complain about much and is seldom depressed.

- tries never to disturb people by turning on her stereo too loud or too early in the morning. When she turns on a TV program or buys something like ice cream, she takes other people's tastes into account.

- is always ready to drop what she is doing and play with her four-year-old daughter or help her 11-year-old son with homework and other problems. She spends little on herself but puts all the family's extra money into a savings account for the children's education.

- studies for three hours every evening during the week and for five hours a day on weekends because she wants to get good grades and eventually become a lawyer.

Exercise 2 (approximately 5 minutes). Think of a friend or relative with a personality trait such as generosity, greediness, dishonesty, calmness, etc. Write a description of his or her actions and attitudes illustrating that one trait.

_____

_____

_____

_____

_____

Section 6
Description by Comparison

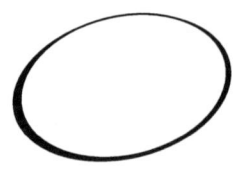

Exercises

Instructions. A good way to help your reader visualize something you are describing is to compare it to something else that is already familiar. This is illustrated in the following exercises.

Exercise 1 (approximately 10 minutes). Number the sentences within each of the three paragraphs to form the best logical order. One sentence has already been numbered, as is the case in some other exercises throughout the Student Workbook.

First Paragraph

____ A kernel of wheat is about the size of a grain of rice.

____ Why is whole wheat bread more nutritious than white bread?

____ But the structure of a wheat kernel can be visualized better by comparing it to something larger and easier to see, such as an egg.

____ To answer this question, it is necessary to examine a kernel of wheat.

Second Paragraph

____ An egg has three parts: shell, white, and yolk.

_3_ Its covering (shell) is called the bran.

____ Thus, the three parts of a wheat kernel are the bran, endosperm, and germ.

____ The counterpart of an egg's yolk is called the kernel's germ.

____ That which corresponds to the white of an egg is called the endosperm of a wheat kernel.

____ A kernel of wheat also has three parts.

14 Creating Word Pictures

Third Paragraph

___ Only the endosperm is then used to produce white flour for making appealing baked goods.

___ For this reason, whole wheat bread is more nutritious.

___ Therefore, the endosperm is separated from the bran and germ in a process called milling.

___ Bakers have found that the endosperm makes the smoothest, tastiest bread and cake.

___ Unfortunately, the bran and germ contain more vitamins, fiber, and other healthy substances than the endosperm.

___ Whole wheat flour keeps all three parts of the wheat kernel.

Exercise 2 (approximately 10 minutes). Write the sentences in the order you numbered them to form a paper that includes a description of a wheat kernel illustrated through comparison with an egg.

Exercise 3 (approximately 15 minutes). Put away all other material from Exercises 1 and 2. Then write a short paper explaining why white bread is *less* nutritious than whole wheat bread. Include a description of a wheat kernel illustrated through comparison with an egg.

- bran - shell
- endosperm - white
- germ - yolk
- endosperm - used to make white flour for smoother, tastier bread and cake
- milling - separating endosperm from bran and germ
- bran and germ - contain more vitamins, fiber, and other healthy substances

Section 7
The School Cafeteria

Exercises

Instructions. Do you like your school cafeteria? Some school cafeterias are quite good, but others are a disappointment. The following exercises contain a description of a school cafeteria that could use improvement.

Exercise 1 (approximately 10 minutes). In planning a paper on the school cafeteria, the following ideas might come to mind:

- short hours
- long line
- overcooked vegetables
- everything lukewarm
- crowded seating
- disgusting piles of dirty dishes

- stale desserts
- greasy hamburgers
- small portions
- unfriendly staff
- noisy room
- high prices

To organize these ideas into a paper, you could group them into the following categories. Write each item from the above list in an appropriate category. The first item has already been partly written for you.

Poor service in obtaining food: <u>short hours,</u>_____

Poor food: _____

Unpleasant atmosphere while eating: _____

Bad value (pay much, get little): _____

Exercise 2 (approximately 15 minutes). Ideas about the cafeteria from the previous exercise are contained in the following sentences. Number the sentences within each paragraph to form the best logical order.

First Paragraph

___ For one thing, the serving hours are too short.

___ This means if you were too rushed to have breakfast, you can't get any food until noon.

___ A second problem is the long waiting line.

___ The cafeteria doesn't open until 12:00 o'clock, and it closes at exactly 1:30.

___ Instead, she dumps the food on your plate as if she resents serving students.
(Vocabulary Tip: resent– become offended and angry.)

___ A third complaint is the unfriendliness of the staff.

___ There is a consensus among students that the school cafeteria stinks.
(Vocabulary Tip: consensus– agreement.)

___ Or if you are busy with a school assignment during the brief period it is open, you totally miss lunch.

___ The lady serving the hot food never smiles.

___ Due partly to the short hours and partly to an inefficient cashier who constantly chats with the lady who makes coffee and replaces desserts, the waiting line is always long and slow.

___ If you only have a half-hour for lunch, there is no point going to the cafeteria because you may not get through the long line in time to eat.

___ Furthermore, the salad lady gets irritated and rude if you ask her to look in the refrigerator for a dish of cottage cheese or something else not available on the shelf.

Second Paragraph

___ It is all the same lukewarm temperature.

___ When you do get your food, you wonder whether the long wait and unpleasant service were worth enduring.
(Vocabulary Tip: endure– suffer, tolerate, put up with.)

___ First, the hot food isn't very hot, and the cold food isn't very cold.

___ The meatloaf is lukewarm, the vegetables are lukewarm, and the jellos and puddings are lukewarm.

___ What makes the food even more tasteless is that the cooked foods are overcooked, and the desserts are usually stale.

___ The string beans and carrots don't have a trace of crispness or sweetness left, as if they were boiled for hours.

___ And the slices of cake are so dry that it is rumored they are bought discounted from a supermarket after sitting on the shelf beyond their expiration date.

___ The buns are crusty with age, while the meat patties are thin as crackers and dripping with grease.

___ Even the old American standby, the hamburger, is a total loss.

Third Paragraph

___ The unavoidable conclusion is that the cafeteria requires new management to make it an efficient, pleasant place to eat.

___ A Pepsi costs 75¢ and a hamburger $2, while a store down the block charges 50¢ for the same size soda and $1.50 for a better burger.

___ Also, the conveyor belt where you are supposed to place dirty dishes is often backed up, creating a disgusting pile of trays, encrusted plates, and spilled food.

___ The tables are cramped together, so you hear all the conversations and noise from kids at other tables.

___ The atmosphere in the cafeteria is another disappointment.

_6_ Furthermore, the servings are minuscule, especially the meat portions which are about the size of the children's portions sold at reduced prices in other cafeterias.
(Vocabulary Tip: minuscule– tiny.)

___ Added to all of this are the outrageous prices.

Exercise 3 (approximately 15 minutes). Write the sentences in the order you numbered them to form a paper describing an unappealing school cafeteria.

_____

_____

_____

_____

_____

Exercise 4 (approximately 15 minutes). Write a paper about a *good* cafeteria. You may use the paper from exercise 3 as a model by changing bad characteristics to good ones. For instance, you can change long lines and bad service to short lines and quick, friendly service. Or you can use your own words and experiences.

Section 8
Steel Drums from Striking Hands

Exercises

Instructions. The sounds, sights, and impressions that a writer experienced as she became acquainted with steel drums and fascinated by the skillful power of a drum-maker's hands are described in the following exercise.

Exercise 1 (approximately 15 minutes). Number the sentences within each of the nine paragraphs to form the best logical order.

First Paragraph

_____ Following the music to its source brought us to the pool deck of one of the hotels and a man playing a set of double tenor steel drums.

_____ Last year my husband and I were walking on the beach when we heard something that sounded like a xylophone or a piano, but more pleasant than either.

_____ I watched my husband's fascination grow as he engaged the musician in a conversation that led to inviting the musician, Walter, and his drums to our house that evening.

Second Paragraph

__3__ George is a pan maker, and my husband decided to call him and order a set.

_____ It was then that we learned about George Richards, Walter's lifelong friend from his native Granada, who now lives about 60 miles from our house.

_____ When he came, he explained that steel drums, or pans as they are called by those who play them, are handmade from 55-gallon steel oil cans and cannot be purchased at any department or music store.

Third Paragraph

_____ However, he understood that we wanted a set of steel drums as soon as possible.

_____ His words, bathed in a rich Caribbean accent, were carried by a voice so soft that they were almost lost in the lilting island tones.
(*Vocabulary Tip: lilt– rhythm, with fluctuating pitch.*)

22 *Creating Word Pictures*

___ Talking with George on the telephone was difficult.

___ And it was only two days plus a few hours past our scheduled meeting that he arrived at our house with a, "Hello, Mon. I made your drum."

Fourth Paragraph

___ A knit cap was pulled over his small ears and down to his neat eyebrows which framed large, sensitive brown eyes that almost squinted shut when he flashed his wide grin.

___ George was dressed in an army-style green coat that hung on his long lanky frame to the middle of the calves of his legs.

___ His teeth were in straight rows and seemed even whiter against his dark skin and short, black beard and mustache.

Fifth Paragraph

_2_ His neatly shaved brown head nearly touched the ceiling as he explained that he had to "find the notes in the pans."

___ Bent at the waist with his right ear close to the pan, he began to strike each note until it sounded as he thought it should.

___ He then borrowed our ball-peen hammer to tune the drums.

_5_ Smoke encircled the whole scene as he puffed constantly on his Kool cigarette.

___ After the drums were set up in the house, George removed his coat and hat.

___ Occasionally the end of the cigarette would fall into the pans, but his concentration never faltered as the ashes danced to the vibrations.

Sixth Paragraph

___ As he tuned the drums, I noticed his wide hands, which seemed too big to be carried even by his muscular arms.

___ After every other strike of the hammer, he would force each note smooth with the tips of the long, brawny fingers of his left hand.

_4_ While I watched this process, I was amazed at the strength and genius his hands represented.

_2_ He struck the metal over and over again, with the hammer held so tightly in his right hand that his dark skin paled at the knuckles as the bones pushed against his taut flesh.

Seventh Paragraph

___ I went back into the house when I heard him begin to play chords.

___ The pounding of the hammer finally drove me outdoors.

___ He greeted me with, "See, I made you good pans."

___ I do not know how George stood the noise, but he didn't stop until each of the 30 notes sounded as they should.

Eighth Paragraph

___ It was then that I understood why our telephone conversations with George were so difficult to understand: I needed to see his hands; they made everything clear.

___ Every word was expressed with a gesture that accented its meaning.

___ When we talked about music and his life in Granada, my attention was again drawn to his hands.

___ I realized that just as they held the secret to making the pans, they also held the key to understanding his verbal communication.

Ninth Paragraph

___ Several times we have given him a call, and he has returned, maybe not just when expected because he travels to various parts of the country "touching up" drums that he has made.

___ Before George left that night he promised to come back whenever the drums needed tuning.

___ However, he eventually gets back to us, and we are always glad for the chance to once again observe his magic hands at work.

___ "Just give me a call, Mon. I'll get back to you," he promised.

Exercise 2 (approximately 15 minutes). Write the sentences in the order you numbered them to form a paper describing sounds, sights, and impressions experienced in becoming acquainted with steel drums and George the drum-maker.

Section 9
Analysis of Creating Word Pictures

The exercises in this chapter illustrated how word pictures can be "painted" of people and situations. In writing descriptions, remember that "describe" means to tell about something in detail. Good descriptions capture the sensations of the scene being written about: sights, sounds, smells, tastes, and feelings—both physical and emotional. Your readers will only see, hear, and feel the experiences you are describing if you present enough details for them to recreate the experiences in their own minds. Without these details, they are left staring at a blank screen.

Sections 6 and 8 showed how a description can take the form of a comparison with something familiar. In 8, the sound of steel drums was conveyed by comparing it to the sound of a piano or xylophone. Section 6 portrayed the structure of a tiny wheat kernel by comparing it part-by-part to the more familiar structure of an egg. Such comparisons provide the reader with a link between the unknown and the known.

Try to be systematic in your descriptions. For the buffet table (Section 2), the description began at the far right with the plates and progressed systematically until the silverware was reached at the far left. The cafeteria description in Section 7 began with the short hours, then followed a path through the serving line, past the food, and into the dining area. The description of the wheat kernel was introduced with the statement, "An egg has three parts: shell, white, and yolk." Then the description of the kernel followed the same order: bran, endosperm, and germ. Being systematic like this makes it much easier for a reader to follow and visualize your description.

Finally, when you are looking for the right word to convey some impression, you might find a thesaurus handy. A thesaurus is a book listing synonyms (words of similar meaning) and antonyms (opposite meaning). This special type of dictionary can lead you to just the word for making a description vivid. If you do not own a thesaurus, you can buy one for a reasonable price at a paperback bookstore.

Exercises for writing your own original descriptions will be given in the next chapter, after a brief discussion of how writers actually write.

Chapter 2
The Writing Process

In the last chapter you numbered sentences and then wrote them into papers. It is important to understand that the authors of this book were not able to just sit down and write these papers in their final form the way you did. Instead, like most other writers, they went through a series of stages.

First, writers have or develop a general idea about a topic. Bringing to mind related facts and examples, they talk to themselves as if they were telling someone else everything they consider important on the subject. They do research in encyclopedias or other reference sources if additional information is needed. And they may brainstorm to bring many ideas to mind quickly (brainstorming is discussed later). This stage of writing can be done individually or in groups.

After organizing their ideas mentally, writers generally find it useful to write a rough outline, emphasizing major points and examples. As writers talk to and among themselves in outlining a paper, they may try to think of good sentences to introduce or explain ideas. When a good sentence comes to mind, it is written down immediately so it will not be forgotten. (Thinking up good sentences is hard work!) Sometimes entire paragraphs are written this way and saved for later use in the paper. In addition, useful ideas and examples that are not yet in sentence form are written down and saved to be placed in the proper spot after writing has begun.

Then writers begin their actual papers. Often new ideas come to mind as they write, and these are added to the ideas already in the outline. After writing several sentences or paragraphs, writers may stop to read over their material. Quite frequently, they see better ways to express ideas, so they delete or scratch out phrases or sentences and rewrite them. Gradually, writers work through all the ideas in the outline until the paper is completed.

But experienced writers know they are still not done. This is just the first draft. Writers have found that when they read a paper that they have written just once, they almost always discover ways to revise and improve it. Of course spelling and grammar errors are discovered and corrected. But the most important reason for revising is to express meaning more clearly. A writer may discover that his or her meaning is vague at certain points or that he or she has not fully explained relationships among ideas. Often such lack of clarity is seen only after a paper has been completed and the writer reads it from start to finish with a fresh eye.

A second purpose for revising is to improve word choice. Frequently, in reading through a completed paper, the writer thinks of better words to use. The writer might change "very large" to "gigantic" or "umpire in the game of baseball" to "baseball umpire." He or she looks for places where more powerful words or compact phrases can be used.

A third purpose for revising is to improve sentence structure. A writer might find that he or she has written one short sentence after another, with no long sentences to change the pace. Or the writer might find he or she has started five sentences in a row with the same word or subject, giving a repetitive, boring quality to the writing. Such problems are corrected by rewriting several sentences so they don't all start the same way or have the same length.

A fourth purpose for revising is that, as a writer reads through the first draft, he or she often thinks of new ideas or illustrations to enrich or clarify the paper. Many writers report that their papers continue to improve as they reread and revise them three and even four times. Books (including this one) are often revised dozens of times. Revising is an important part of writing. With your own writing, it is to your advantage to never submit a paper without first reading it through, correcting spelling or grammar errors, and revising wherever necessary.

In summary, writing a paper generally involves these stages:

1. Thinking of ideas: talking to yourself about the topic as if you were explaining it to someone else (or actually sharing your ideas with someone else), doing research in encyclopedias and other sources, perhaps brainstorming to get many ideas quickly.

2. Organizing ideas: making an outline or thinking of sentences to introduce and express ideas.

3. Writing a first draft.

4. Revising: adding ideas, expressing ideas more clearly, using more powerful language, improving sentences, correcting spelling and grammar errors.

5. Revising again—preferably after not reading the paper for at least a day: fresh ideas come to mind for explaining and expressing thoughts, and awkward or unclear sections may only be recognized after a time lapse.

Section 1
Describe Things on a Wall

Exercise

Instructions. The exercise below asks you to describe a wall with things on it. You will have to organize the description systematically and write sentences that clearly describe the shapes and positions of the objects. After writing the first draft, read it over carefully. Of course, correct spelling and grammar errors. In addition, you will probably find sentences that can be revised to make them sound better or describe the objects more clearly.

Exercise (approximately 15 minutes). Describe the wall shown below. Rather than moving from one end to the other, as in the buffet table/food bar paper, you might start at the door and first move to the left, then to the right. Remember to describe the shapes of things (with words like "triangular" and "arched-shaped") as well as their sizes and locations. Use this and the next page to write your description. After writing a first draft, read it over to correct spelling and grammar errors and also to describe the wall more clearly.

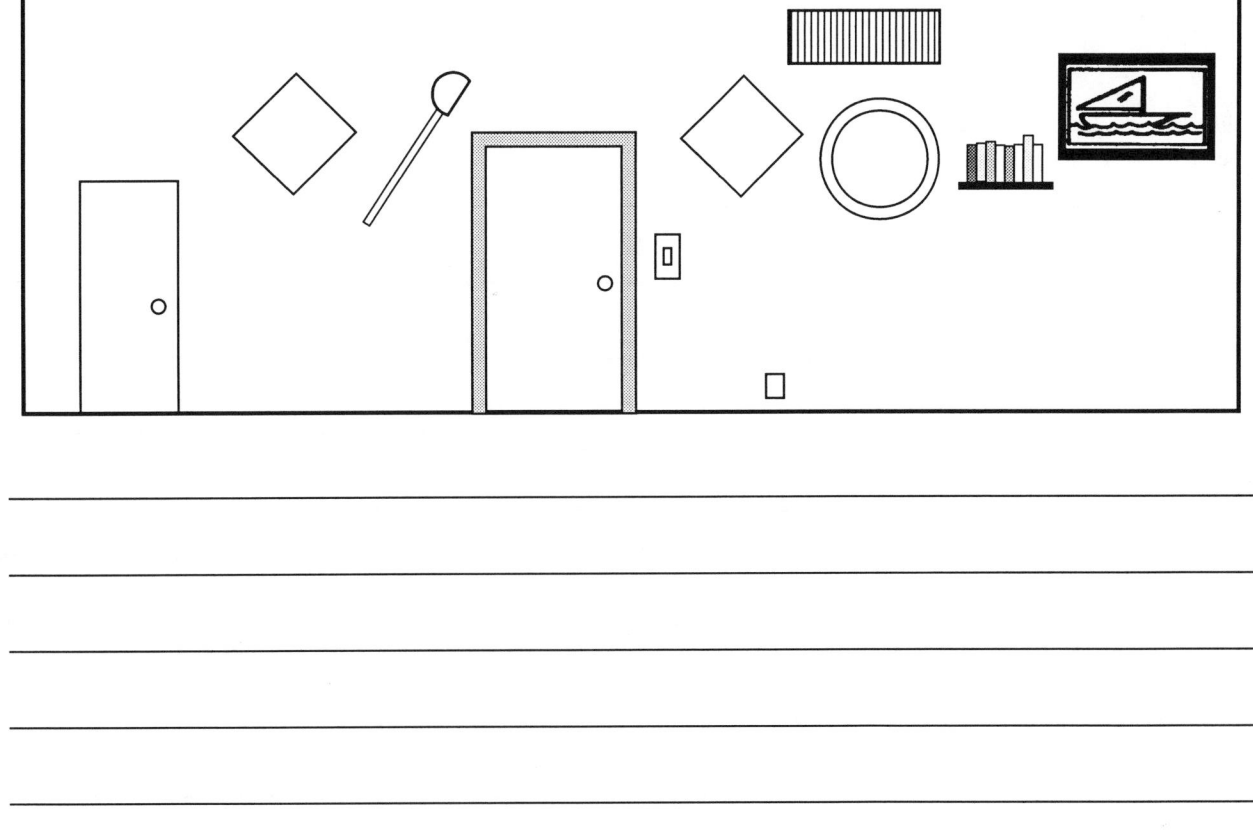

_____

_____

_____

_____

The Whimbey Writing Program - Student Workbook

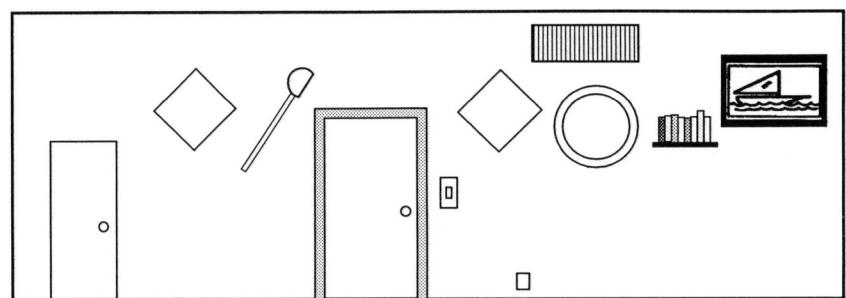

Section 2
Describe Yourself

Exercise

Exercise (approximately 20 minutes). Write a physical description of yourself in approximately 150 words. This requires thinking of the characteristics you want to describe, organizing the description, and finding the right words to express your thoughts. Because this is a more difficult writing task than that of Section 1, you can expect to do more revising before you have a well-written description of yourself. Include physical characteristics such as overall size and body type along with details about eye and hair color, hair style, etc. Also describe what you are now wearing, with details about clothes color, design, etc. After writing a first draft, read it over to improve the description of yourself in any way possible and also to correct spelling and grammar errors.

Section 3
Where are You Now?

Exercise

Exercise (approximately 20 minutes). Write a 150-word description of the room you are in now. Include furniture and objects on walls.

Section 4
Buy a Car or Furnish a Room

Exercise

Exercise (approximately 30 minutes). Pick one of the following topics to write about:

- Assume you have unlimited funds to design an automobile. Write a 200-word description of your ideal car, including details like body style, color, seats, dashboard, sound system, engine, and other equipment. You might begin by brainstorming: think of everything you could possibly want in or on a car.

OR

- Assume you have unlimited funds to design your own living room (or bedroom). Write a 200-word description of this ideal room, including details such as view, shape, walls, rug, furniture, lighting, mirrors, electronic equipment, etc. You might begin by brainstorming; let your imagination run wild. List lots of wall colors, window styles, views, wallpaper designs, furniture—everything that comes to mind. You might get additional ideas by recalling beautiful rooms you have visited or seen in magazines and movies.

_____
_____
_____
_____
_____
_____
_____
_____
_____

Section 5
What Do You Want to Do?

Exercise

Exercise (approximately 15 minutes). What career might you be interested in pursuing? Write a 100-word description of that career in terms of two or three characteristics important to you. Here are examples of job characteristics people consider: type of work, salary, working conditions, hours, training or educational requirements, chance for advancement, vacations, travel, and job security. Write a detailed description of two or three such characteristics for your career.

Chapter 3
Describing a Sequence of Actions or Events

Writing often takes the form of describing a series of actions or events. One example is a history textbook, which recounts the events considered important during some time period. Another example is a description of the events occurring on a trip, over the course of a day, or even during a fight between two angry cats.

Sometimes in describing a series of events you say that one event caused another. History books, for example, devote much space and thought to tracing the sequence of events that led to major wars. At times you may show how one event caused a second event that, in turn, had still another effect, forming a cause-effect chain. Exercises in this unit illustrate several writing patterns for presenting cause-effect relations.

Another type of paper that relates a series of actions is called a "process" paper. A process paper describes how something is accomplished, such as the process of passing a federal law in the United States. Somewhat similar to the process paper is the instructions paper, which tells the reader how he or she can do something like make pancake batter or program a VCR. An instructions paper is generally more detailed than a process paper because its purpose is to tell the reader how to perform every step himself or herself.

All the papers in this unit share the common element of describing actions or events occurring over time. Descriptions of events occurring over time often use words and phrases such as *before, after, two hours later, in 1995, first, second, next, then,* and *finally*. Cause-effect descriptions use *because, since, therefore, so, consequently,* and *result*. Note how such terms connect ideas and paragraphs in the papers that follow so you can use them in your own writing.

Section 1
Cause-Effect

When one event precedes another, we sometimes conclude that the first event causes the second. If a person has several drinks in a bar and then drives his or her car into a telephone pole, we may conclude that excessive drinking caused the accident. Of course, we cannot always say that one event causes another just because the first event regularly precedes the second. For example, the 8:00 a.m. train precedes the 8:10 train every morning, but we do not say that the arrival of the 8:00 a.m. train causes the arrival of the later one. However, the exercises in this section are about events with cause-effect relations.

Here is an example of two sentences expressing a cause-effect relationship, which can be combined in a single sentence:

>   Cause: Brian fell asleep smoking.
>   Effect: The bed caught fire.
>   Combined: The bed caught fire because Brian fell asleep smoking.
>   or
>   Because Brian fell asleep smoking, the bed caught fire.

In this section you will analyze and write longer cause-effect descriptions.

Exercises

SET 1. A CHAIN OF CAUSES

Sometimes an action or situation has an effect that causes another effect. This is called a "cause-effect chain" and is illustrated in the following exercises.

Exercise 1 (approximately 5 minutes). Number these sentences on the social security system so the paragraph starts with a cause and then leads to an effect.

___ Consequently, people are living longer and the proportion of the population over age 65 has increased.
(Vocabulary Tip: consequently– as a result.)

___ Because there are now relatively more elderly retirees taking money out of the social security system and fewer working-age people paying into it, the system is threatened with bankruptcy.
(Vocabulary Tip: bankrupt– having no money, out of business.)

___ Medicine has recently conquered many diseases that used to be fatal.
(Vocabulary Tip: fatal– causing death.)

Exercise 2 (approximately 5 minutes). Write the sentences in the order you numbered them to form a paragraph describing a cause-effect chain.

_____

_____

_____

_____

_____

Exercise 3 (approximately 5 minutes). The paragraph you just wrote described a cause-effect chain. Here is the beginning of the chain:

Relationship 1	Cause:	Medicine has recently conquered many diseases that used to be fatal.
	Effect:	People are living longer and the proportion of the population over age 65 has increased.
Relationship 2	Cause:	The proportion of the population over age 65 has increased.
	Effect:	Relatively fewer people are putting money into the social security system, and more are taking money out.
Relationship 3	Cause:	_____
	Effect:	_____

Notice that the effect in Relationship 1 is the cause in Relationship 2. Use complete sentences to fill in the cause and effect for Relationship 3.

The Whimbey Writing Program - Student Workbook

Exercise 4 (approximately 5 minutes). The paragraph you wrote in Exercise 2 began with a cause and ended with an effect. But sometimes you may begin with the effect and then explain its causes. Number the following sentences so they start with the effect and then explain the causes.

___ The result is relatively fewer working-age people paying into the social security system and more elderly retirees taking money out, which is financially unhealthy.

___ Consequently, people are living longer and the proportion of the population over age 65 is increasing.

___ The social security system is threatened with bankruptcy, partly because of progress in medicine.

___ Medical science has recently conquered many diseases that used to be fatal.

Exercise 5 (approximately 5 minutes). Write the sentences in the order you numbered them to form a paragraph describing an effect and its causes.

_____

_____

_____

_____

_____

_____

_____

_____

_____

SET 2. MULTIPLE CAUSES

Sometimes several causes contribute to an effect. For example, excessive speed combined with wet roads might have caused an automobile accident. Another example is shown in these exercises.

Exercise 1 (approximately 5 minutes). The following sentences describe an unfortunate situation and three causes contributing to it. Number the sentences in the best logical order.

___ Finally, because of increased real estate and heating costs, houses and apartments have become smaller.

___ First, the majority of working-age American adults hold jobs, so they don't have time to care for an aged parent.

___ In earlier times, and still in places such as China, the elderly were cared for in the families of their grown children.

___ There is no longer an extra room for Grandma.

___ But this is no longer the case in America for several reasons.

___ Second, American families are highly mobile, moving frequently to obtain better jobs or other benefits.
(*Vocabulary Tip: mobile– moving often, able to move.*)

___ This divides families by hundreds or even thousands of miles, rather than leaving adult children near their elderly parents.

Exercise 2 (approximately 5 minutes). Write the sentences in the order you numbered them to form a paragraph stating a problem and three causes.

_____
_____
_____
_____
_____
_____
_____
_____
_____
_____
_____

The Whimbey Writing Program - Student Workbook

Exercise 3 (approximately 4 minutes). The paragraph you just wrote presented three reasons (causes) why the elderly are not being cared for by their grown children. The paragraph also explained causes behind these three causes. For example, the first cause given was that working-age American adults don't have time to care for aged parents. But this was said to result from something else. State in a complete sentence why working-age American adults don't have time.

Cause: _____

_____

Exercise 4 (approximately 3 minutes). State in a complete sentence why families are divided by great distances.

Cause: _____

_____

Exercise 5 (approximately 3 minutes). State in a complete sentence why there is no longer an extra room for Grandma.

Cause: _____

_____

Exercise 6 (approximately 10 minutes). The chart below is one way to clearly show the cause-effect relationships presented in the paragraph. Several causes and effects have already been written in the chart. Write the missing entries in the spaces provided. Note that Cause 3 has two parts.

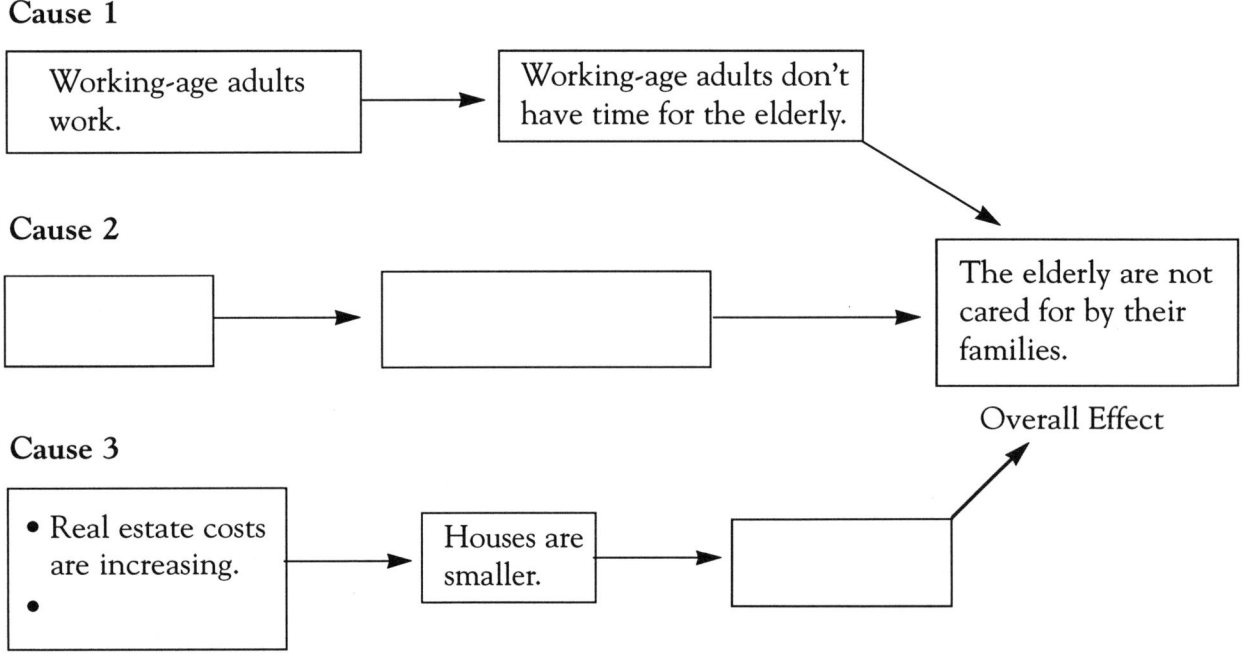

42 Describing a Sequence of Actions or Events

SET 3. ACTION WITH BOTH BAD AND GOOD EFFECTS

Sometimes an action with intended good effects also has bad effects. Among the following sentences, one describes a school action, some describe negative effects of the action, and the remainder explain the positive effects.

Exercise 1 (approximately 5 minutes). Number the following sentences to first describe a school action, then the negative effects, and finally the positive effects.

___ Others, especially parents, complained that the new menus were too expensive.

___ Nutritionists have complained that, under the new system, most students skip the healthy alternatives and eat too much fast food, getting too much fat in their diets.

___ Moreover, the problem of students leaving the campus for lunch has diminished.

___ Now they eat lunch on campus.

___ Over the past few years, schools have broadened their lunch menus by adding salad bars and allowing food from fast-food restaurants to be served to students.

___ But students like the change, saying it gives them more choices for lunch.

___ Many students were not eating the lunches being served and were breaking the rules by leaving campus to get their lunches.

Exercise 2 (approximately 5 minutes). Write the sentences to form a paragraph that begins with a school action, then describe negative results of the action, and finally the positive results.

_____
_____
_____
_____
_____
_____
_____
_____

Exercise 3 (approximately 15 minutes). With all material from the exercises just given out of sight, write a paragraph about any school action that had both negative and positive results. You may write about school lunches, but be sure all material from the exercises is away.

_____
_____
_____
_____
_____
_____
_____
_____
_____
_____

SET 4. "SURE, DEAR"

Do people listen when you talk? The following sentences can be arranged to describe how one person caused another to stop listening.

Exercise 1 (approximately 5 minutes). Number the sentences to form the best logical order.

____ So she sat down with the editorial page and began enjoying a humorous article about the city's mayor.

____ She just replied, "Sure, dear," and read on.

____ A woman decided to test whether her husband heard anything she said when he had his head buried in the paper during breakfast.

____ Without looking up from his paper, he replied automatically, "Yes, dear. Thank you, dear."

____ Serving him some pancakes, she said, "Have several. I filled them with cockroaches."

____ She barely heard her husband when he asked for another piece of toast or something.

44 *Describing a Sequence of Actions or Events*

Exercise 2 (approximately 5 minutes). Write the sentences in the order you numbered them.

Exercise 3 (approximately 15 minutes). With all material from exercises 1 and 2 out of sight, write your own paragraph about a similar experience you have had or make up your own story along the same lines.

SET 5. SMOKING DANGERS

The following sentences can be arranged into a paper describing some dangerous cause-effect relationships.

Exercise 1 (approximately 10 minutes). Number the sentences within each paragraph to form the best logical order.

First Paragraph

____ The tobacco industry responded to these findings by marketing filter cigarettes advertised as lower in tar and nicotine.

____ There are several reasons for this.

____ The tar in cigarettes was identified as the substance producing cancer, while the nicotine was found harmful to the heart and also addictive (causing a person to crave more cigarettes).

____ But recent studies reveal that "low tar and nicotine" cigarettes have not reduced the risk of cancer and heart disease.

____ Around 1960, it was established that smoking cigarettes increased a person's chance of developing cancer and heart disease.

Second Paragraph

____ While both of these flavorings are safe to eat, they can cause cancer when smoked.

____ First, it has been discovered that other substances in cigarettes besides tar and nicotine are also health hazards when burned and inhaled.

____ Simply eliminating the two flavorings would not solve the problem because there are about 2,000 other chemicals (such as dangerous carbon monoxide) which are produced by a burning cigarette.

____ For example, cigarette manufacturers add licorice and sugar to improve the flavor of cigarettes.

Third Paragraph

____ For example, he may inhale more deeply and hold the smoke longer.

____ Through this misunderstanding, he will inhale a greater amount of other dangerous chemicals than he would by smoking a smaller number of regular cigarettes.

46 Describing a Sequence of Actions or Events

___ Or he may smoke more cigarettes per day, believing that "low tar and nicotine" cigarettes are safe and can be smoked in large quantity without risk.

___ A second reason is that once a person is addicted to nicotine, he finds ways to obtain the amount of nicotine his body craves, even with low nicotine cigarettes.

Fourth Paragraph

___ In fact, a report in the medical journal *Lancet* stated that the risk of heart attack was just as high for a group of filter-cigarette smokers as for regular-cigarette smokers.

___ To stamp out the cancer and heart disease still being caused by smoking, people must be made aware of these dangers.

___ For these and other reasons, it is now believed that no cigarettes are safe.

Exercise 2 (approximately 10 minutes). Write the sentences in the order you numbered them to form a paper explaining some of the cause-effect relationships that make low tar and nicotine cigarettes unsafe.

Section 2
Describing a Process and Giving Instructions

A great deal of practical writing takes the form of explaining how something is done or telling the reader exactly how he or she can do something. In this section, the first set of exercises involves a brief general description of the law-making process. From reading this description a person gets an overview of how laws are made, although the selection does not present enough details for a person to actually go through all the steps of making a law. By contrast, the second set of exercises involves instructions for baking cornbread that are detailed enough to allow you to bake this special bread yourself. When you do Set 2, notice how the instructions present every step in order. Poor instructions sometimes confuse people by jumping back and forth among the steps.

Exercises

SET 1. DESCRIBING A PROCESS: LAWMAKING

Exercise 1 (approximately 5 minutes). Number the following sentences in the best logical order.

___ A bill vetoed by the President could still become a law, but it would have to return to Congress and receive a two-thirds favorable vote, so this occurs infrequently.
(*Vocabulary Tip: Congress– Senate and House of Representatives.*)

___ If the President signs it, then it becomes a law for the whole country.

___ If the committee approves the bill (often only with modifications), it is presented to the entire House and Senate for a vote.
(*Vocabulary Tips: bill– draft (rough copy) of a proposed law; modifications– changes.*)

___ First, a senator or member of the House of Representatives introduces a bill, which is assigned to a committee (e.g., Labor Committee) for study and discussion.

___ The bill must receive a majority of the votes in both the House and Senate in order to be passed on to the President for his signature or veto.
(*Vocabulary Tips: majority– more than half; veto– a "no" vote.*)

___ However, if he casts a veto, the bill generally dies.

___ Making a new federal law applying to the entire United States requires a number of steps.

Exercise 2 (approximately 5 minutes). Write the sentences in the order you numbered them to describe the process of making a new federal law.

_____

_____

_____

_____

_____

_____

_____

_____

_____

SET 2. GRANDMA'S CORNBREAD

Good cooks have secrets that make their dishes especially delicious. If you want to prepare one of their specialties, you must follow their procedure exactly. Here is an example.

Exercise 1 (approximately 10 minutes). Number the sentences within each paragraph to form the best logical order.

First Paragraph

____ The magic lay in knowing exactly how Grandma used those simple ingredients.

____ Many people "stopped by" around supper time just to watch her make this special bread because they had learned from their own failures that just knowing the ingredients was not enough.

____ When my grandmother was alive, she was one of the best cooks in our county and famous for baking that old-time staple, cornbread.
(*Vocabulary Tip: staple– a basic food like sugar or butter.*)

Second Paragraph

___ She said you couldn't use just any pan to bake cornbread with such a crispy, golden-brown crust that it flipped onto a plate without leaving even a crumb behind.

___ Using an unseasoned pan resulted in clumps of cornbread sticking to the sides, according to Grandma.

___ This seasoning process was repeated three times before the skillet became "the skillet" for baking cornbread; it was never used for anything else, and it was never washed.

___ Then she put it away until the next day when she again rubbed it with grease and baked it in the oven.

___ To season her iron skillet, Grandma rubbed grease onto the inside and outside of the skillet and put it into a hot (400 degrees) oven to bake for 15 minutes.

___ Grandma's first secret was her "seasoned" ten-inch iron skillet.

Third Paragraph

__3__ The remaining steps were simple, but if they weren't followed in sequence, the cornbread would turn lumpy or rise unevenly in the skillet.

___ This dry mixture was stirred together by hand for about two minutes to make sure everything was mixed evenly.

___ At the same time, she greased the inside of the skillet and put it on a stove burner set for low heat so the skillet would be smoky hot when the cornbread batter was poured in later.

___ In actually making the cornbread, Grandma first preheated the oven to 450 degrees.

___ Into a large bowl Grandma put one cup of flour, one cup of cornmeal, one teaspoon of sugar, 1/2 teaspoon of salt, and four teaspoons of baking powder.

___ Finally, one cup of buttermilk was stirred into the batter to make it moist and to give the cornbread its rich taste.

Fourth Paragraph

___ When the timer rang, Grandma took the skillet from the oven and pressed a plate to the top of it, flipped them over, and lifted off the skillet to reveal a golden, delicious-smelling cake of cornbread.

___ The batter was poured into the slightly smoking skillet, which was then placed in the hot oven for 20 minutes.

Exercise 2 (approximately 10 minutes). Write the sentences in the order you numbered them to form a description of the procedure Grandma used to make cornbread.

Exercise 3 (approximately 15 minutes). Rewrite the procedure for baking Grandma's cornbread as instructions to the reader (i.e., a recipe) rather than a description of Grandma's activities. Tell the reader what he or she should do. You could start like this:

> To bake great cornbread you must first have a "seasoned" skillet. Rub grease on the inside and outside of a ten-inch iron skillet. Then put it into a hot . . . .

Section 3
Narrating a Series of Events

The remaining exercises in this unit illustrate some of the language and logic that may be used in describing any series of events.

Exercises

SET 1. WORDS SHOWING SEQUENCE

Exercise (approximately 5 minutes). In writing a paper about a series of actions, you often use words like "first," "next," and "after" to show sequence or order. Below are six such words used to tie together sentences describing a series of actions. Use each word only once in filling the blanks for the paragraph that follows.

Next   At   Then   When   After   First

My alarm wakes me every weekday at 7:00 a.m. _____ I shower and shave. _____ I select my clothes for the day and get dressed. _____ I eat breakfast. _____ breakfast I read the paper. _____ my dad is ready, I leave with him for school. _____ 8:30 I begin classes.

SET 2. VARY YOUR SENTENCE PATTERNS

If every sentence in a history paper began: "In 1783 . . . ," "In 1803 . . . ," "In 1819 . . . ," the paper would seem dull and place more importance on dates than on the events and people that made the dates memorable. One way to vary such sentences is to change the position of the date. The date can be placed near the beginning, near the middle, or near the end of a sentence. For example:

Date Near Beginning: In the early 1980s, the first AIDS cases began to appear in the U.S.

Date Near Middle: The first AIDS cases began in the early 1980s to appear in the U.S.

Date Near End: The first AIDS cases began to appear in the U.S. in the early 1980s.

Another way to give the date of an event is to tell how many years it occurred after another event, as shown below.

> Dull: In 1980, Reagan was elected president. In 1984, Reagan was again elected president.
>
> Better: In 1980, Reagan was elected president. <u>Four years later</u> Reagan was again elected president.

Use these sentence patterns in the following exercise.

Exercise (approximately 5 minutes). Following are six sentences all beginning with a date. Rewrite them as a paragraph with varying sentence patterns. Let the first sentence and only one other sentence have the date at the beginning. For the others, have at least one sentence with the date near the middle, at least one with the date near the end, and one with the date given as the number of years following another date.

> In 1776, the 13 original colonies declared their independence from Britain and became the United States.
>
> In 1783, the U.S. obtained most of the territory between the Appalachian Mountains and the Mississippi River through a treaty with Britain.
>
> In 1803, Napoleon sold the Louisiana Territory to the U.S. for $15 million.
>
> In 1819, Florida was purchased from Spain.
>
> In 1845, the citizens of Texas (at that time a separate country) voted to join the United States.
>
> In 1853, additional land in the Southwest was acquired through the Gadsden Purchase.

_____

_____

_____

_____

_____

_____

_____

_____

_____

SET 3. THE PRACTICAL "UN" JOKER

The following sentences can be arranged into a story relating several humorous incidents.

Exercise 1 (approximately 10 minutes). Number the sentences in the best logical order.

____ But Uncle Fred just turned on the lamp switch and began reading his paper in the dark as if nothing were wrong.

____ That is, until we spent a week visiting our Uncle Fred at his ranch.

____ By the time we finished those sandwiches, we had our fill of practical jokes.

____ When Uncle Fred came back, he cracked the eggs into a bowl and, as if nothing unusual had happened, he stirred in a spoonful of mayonnaise.

____ When my sister and I were kids, we loved playing practical jokes.

____ On the first evening we took the bulb out of the lamp by his chair.

____ Then he sprinkled some on our corn flakes and told us to eat all of our cereal if we wanted to go horseback riding with him later.

____ When Uncle Fred came to breakfast, he sprinkled two spoons of it on his corn flakes and began eating without blinking an eye.

____ We were surprised but not crushed, so the next morning we tiptoed into the kitchen before Uncle Fred and filled the sugar bowl with salt.

____ Uncle Fred received a phone call just as he began making egg salad sandwiches for our lunch.

____ We tried just one more trick.

____ With his back turned, we substituted uncooked eggs for the hard boiled ones he had placed on the table.

____ Then he spread the slimy mixture onto some bread, served us the "egg salad" sandwiches, and watched while we ate them.

Exercise 2 (approximately 10 minutes). Write the sentences in the order you numbered them. You may divide the sentences into two or three paragraphs if you prefer.

_____
_____
_____
_____
_____
_____
_____
_____
_____
_____
_____
_____
_____
_____
_____
_____
_____

SET 4. SMOKING ADDICTION   SMOKING

The following sentences can be arranged to describe a series of events marking the ruin of a famous person's health by smoking addiction.

Exercise 1 (approximately 5 minutes). Number the sentences in the best logical order.

___   Next, Freud developed cancer of the mouth.

___ But soon he resumed, describing his craving as "the torture being beyond human power to bear."

___ His first danger signal was the development of an irregular heartbeat accompanied by severe chest pains whenever he smoked.

___ Freud smoked about 20 cigars a day.

___ An illustration of how severe an addiction to tobacco can become is seen in the tragic life of Sigmund Freud, the father of modern psychiatry.
(*Vocabulary Tip: psychiatry— branch of medicine specializing in mental illness.*)

___ The chest pains caused him to swear off cigars temporarily, but shortly he began smoking one a day, then two, and gradually built back up to his full-scale addiction.

___ On the advice of a physician he stopped smoking for a while to halt the cancer.

___ But still Freud smoked, until the cancer finally took his life.

___ The consequence was 33 jaw operations over 16 years, ending with Freud's jaw being totally removed and replaced by a painful mechanical jaw.

Exercise 2 (approximately 5 minutes). Write the sentences in the order you numbered them to form a description of how smoking addiction ruined Freud's health.

_____
_____
_____
_____
_____
_____
_____
_____
_____
_____

SET 5. BITING RAGE

Can you recall and describe a series of events leading to an incident that left you shocked, injured, and more cautious afterward? The following sentences can be arranged to tell such a story.

Exercise 1 (approximately 10 minutes). Number the sentences within each paragraph so they sound best to you. You may discover more than one good arrangement for some paragraphs.

First Paragraph

____ After almost 12 years of treating this animal as if he were a child—caring for him during his illnesses, providing him with the best of food, holding him for countless hours, and loving him as a faithful companion—he bit me as if I were a total stranger.

____ Although it was not as serious as a disease or a life-threatening accident, it has caused me much physical pain and mental anguish.
(*Vocabulary Tip: anguish– intense pain, especially of mind.*)

____ My cat bit me.

____ Last summer I had a painful, scarring experience.

Second Paragraph

____ He was involved in a fight with another cat.

____ And I had been warned many times about the consequences of interfering in such a confrontation.
(*Vocabulary Tip: confrontation– face-to-face meeting of enemies.*)

____ By the time I arrived they were fighting and rolling on a neighbor's porch like characters out of a western movie.

____ Nevertheless, at the first howls of battle, I went to rescue him.

____ My screams to stop were ignored; they continued to fight.

____ Even falling from the porch onto hard concrete did not deter them for a moment.
(*Vocabulary Tip: deter– stop, delay.*)

____ I admit that I was not blameless in the incident.

Third Paragraph

___ Eventually they came to a momentary standoff under a red van.
(*Vocabulary Tip: momentary— lasting just a moment.*

___ Then I picked him up and headed toward home.

___ As I tried to coax my cat out, the other cat broke his stance and ran into the underbrush of a neighboring yard.

___ He purred and rubbed against my leg.

___ Then I felt his fangs puncture my flesh and sink deeper and deeper until they struck bone.

___ I bent down and patted him affectionately, noting scratches on his ears and nose that would be scars for life.

___ I followed them across the street as they chased each other under and between parked cars.

___ I tried to drop him, but I moved too slowly.

___ All at once his body stiffened and a threatening growl came from deep inside his throat.

___ My cat followed, but suddenly, as if bored by the whole thing, he returned to where I was standing.

___ He twisted around in my arms, and I felt his mouth close around my wrist.

Fourth Paragraph

___ When he finally let go, blood flowed down the front and back of my hand as it began swelling to twice its normal size.

___ It throbbed with pain; only thoughts of the need to clean the wounds got me to my feet again.

___ Fourteen pounds of unleashed fury hung from my wrist.

___ I fell to my knees and slung my arm, trying to get him to release me.

Fifth Paragraph

___ I still could not believe that my cat had attacked me so viciously.

___ The pain was constant, but that was minor compared to the mental agony I was suffering.
(Vocabulary Tips: minor– unimportant; agony– intense pain of mind or body.)

___ For three days my wrist and palm were so swollen that I could not open or close my hand.

___ Those other owners probably held the same belief, until their pets reacted to instincts, temporarily blinded and out of control.
(Vocabulary Tips: instincts– inborn drives; temporarily– for a short period of time.)

___ I had heard horror stories about other animals attacking their owners, but I had been sure that our relationship was different, stronger.

Sixth Paragraph

___ Oh, I still pat him, feed him, let him sit at my feet, but I do not pick him up and hold him in my arms—not yet.

___ Of that part I remain very fearful.

___ The scars on our relationship are also permanent.

___ I still love him, but I do not trust that part of his being that denied the existence of our relationship.

___ Today my wrist has four puncture scars that will be there forever.

Exercise 2 (approximately 15 minutes). Write the sentences in the order you numbered them to form a story about the series of events that left the writer with a lingering fear of animals.

_____

_____

_____

_____

_____

Section 4
Analysis of Describing a Series of Events or Actions

Section 1 illustrated descriptions of cause-effect relationships. A writer may first describe a cause and then the effect it produced, or the effect may be described first and then its causes (Set 1). If several causes contributed to an effect, these can be described systematically (Set 2). And when one event causes a second event which, in turn, has still another effect, the entire cause-effect chain can be described (Set 1).

Section 2 showed how to describe a process or give a series of instructions. Set 1 involved a brief description of the law-making process. Obviously this was not intended to be detailed instructions for the reader to follow; it only provided a general outline of how a federal law is made.

Set 2 was different. It described Grandma's cornbread-making process in enough detail that a person with a little kitchen experience could actually bake it. In Exercise 3 you were asked to rewrite the description of Grandma's activities as direct instructions for a reader. Think of the types of instructions you see regularly. Every appliance and machine you use—from a hair dryer to an automobile—comes with operating instructions. Instructions also are found in cookbooks, tax forms, home repair manuals—the list is endless. People were paid to write all of these instructions, so you can see that the ability to write clear instructions is valuable. The key to writing good instructions is describing every step the reader must take, in sequence. Remember that you will not be there to explain instructions or other information you write to others. You must be able to describe the steps in the correct order and in a form that can be easily understood.

Generally the sentences used for instructions are grammatically different from most sentences because they do not contain a subject. Compare these two sentences.

- Grandma greased the inside of a pan.

  Subject Verb

- (Implied) Grease the inside of a pan.

  No Subject Verb

In the first sentence the subject is "Grandma." The second sentence does not actually contain a subject, although the implied subject is "you." If the implied subject (you) were included, the sentence would look like this:

You grease the inside of a pan.

Subject Verb

In writing instructions, the word "you" is only included occasionally and sometimes not at all. Notice in the following three sentences that "you" is included only in the opening sentence:

> First you should buckle your seatbelt. Then check that the transmission lever is in neutral or park. Place the square key into the ignition switch on the steering post and turn to the "start" position.

The word "you" could also be deleted from the opening sentence like this: First buckle your seatbelt.

The street directions that you wrote in Section 1 of Chapter 1 were a form of instructions. As you can see from that example, along with the cornbread exercise and the above excerpt from an automobile operator's manual, the sentences used in instructions are generally simple and direct. Whenever you read a set of instructions, pay special attention to the writing style so that you too can write clear instructions for others to follow.

The last section of exercises illustrated patterns for describing series of events. Whenever you tell a story about things that happened to you or someone else, you are describing a series of events. With practice you can develop skill writing such descriptions in personal letters, short stories, and perhaps someday even a best-selling novel. Read short stories, biographies, and novels to see the language and patterns employed by successful writers, learn to recognize the techniques the authors use, and practice them in your own writing.

Section 5
Independent Writing

In doing the following assignments, remember that good writers generally read through and revise a paper TWO or THREE times before considering it finished. After you write a first draft, read it from the beginning and revise sentences that can be expressed more clearly or smoothly. Also add any new ideas and examples you can think of. REWRITE THE WHOLE PAPER IF NECESSARY. Finally, read your paper once more to catch spelling and grammatical errors.

Exercises

Exercise 1 (approximately 15 minutes). Write instructions that will teach a friend how to play your favorite game. Or, write instructions telling a friend how to change a tire, fry an egg, make pancake batter, or do some other task. You might begin by making a list of all the equipment used and every step involved. Then organize the steps into the correct sequence from first to last. Include enough detail about the steps so that the reader understands your instructions. After writing the first draft, read it through, correct spelling/grammar errors, and revise it as necessary to make the instructions clearer. If possible, give it to a classmate to read, and rewrite any portion of the instructions that is unclear.

Exercise 2 (approximately 20 minutes). Describe (minimum 150 words) a series of actions you took (like driving to school) or events you experienced or witnessed today. This might have occurred before you left home, while traveling somewhere, at a restaurant, etc. If any cause-effect relationships were involved, describe them fully. If you have trouble thinking of something to write about, try brainstorming for one minute. Brainstorming means letting as many ideas as possible come into your mind and writing them down quickly without judging or trying to organize them. Think of everything you did and saw since you woke up this morning and write it all down as it comes to mind. Do not try to write complete sentences; just get something on paper for each idea so you will not forget it. The beginning of a brainstorming list might look like this:

> went to Exxon for gas, self-service pump broken, full-service pump was $1.29 for super unleaded, asked attendant if I could get it for self-service price if I pumped it, no, said company wouldn't allow it, went to Amoco, had trouble with cashier . . . .

After brainstorming for one minute, pick some series of actions or events to write about. Do not worry if it is not exciting or funny. Just describe it well for your readers.

_____

Exercise 3 (approximately 15 minutes). Write a 100-word paragraph explaining two causes or reasons for one of the following situations:

- The air is becoming polluted.
- Many Americans are overweight.
- Many high school graduates go (or do not go) to college.
- Many junior high students drop out of school.
- Many women, both single and married, hold jobs.

Begin by describing the situation and one or two examples, such as an example of air pollution. Then describe the two causes, including details or illustrations. If you have trouble thinking of ideas, try brainstorming. Pick one topic. Then take a full minute to write down all examples, causes or reasons, illustrations of causes, and other ideas that come into your mind.

_____

Chapter 4
Organizing Ideas into Patterns: Classification and General-Specific

This chapter introduces two of the most widely used patterns for organizing ideas. Section 1 describes classification and Section 2 covers general-specific. As you work through the exercises, you may notice that the two patterns are like two sides of a coin. On the surface they look different, but their underlying logic is the same. This is explained more at the end of the chapter.

Section 1
Classification

We often group things into categories or classes. This is called *classification*. For example, food could be classified as American, Chinese, Italian, and so on as shown.

Topic: Food

    Category 1: American
        Example 1: hot dog
        Example 2: corn on the cob

    Category 2: Chinese
        Example 1: chow mein
        Example 2: egg foo young

Category 3: Italian
    Example 1: pizza
    Example 2: spaghetti

Category 4: French, etc.

Note that "food" is listed at the top. It is the topic for the classification. Food includes all the examples listed below it. Next are the categories of food, such as American and Chinese. Within each category are examples. Try the following sample exercise on classification.

Sample Exercise. The list of things on the left can be organized into the classification pattern shown on the right. First, read through the entire list and find the topic that includes everything else; write it in the space labeled Topic. Then fill in the three categories and the examples for each category. Complete the exercise before reading the answer, which appears on p. 78. (Hint: cross out each item on the left as you write it in the outline.)

	Topic: _____
trucks	Category 1: _____
trains	Example: _____
land transportation vehicles	Example: _____
transportation vehicles	Example: _____
submarines	Example: _____
jet passenger planes	Example: _____
helicopters	Example: _____
canoes	Category 2: _____
sailboats	Example: _____
bicycles	Example: _____
automobiles	Example: _____
air transportation vehicles	Example: _____
ocean liners	Example: _____
spacecraft	Example: _____
motorcycles	Category 3: _____
small private planes	Example: _____
buses	Example: _____
water transportation vehicles	Example: _____
motorboats and motorized yachts	Example: _____
	Example: _____
	Example: _____

Organizing Ideas into Patterns

Exercises

Exercise 1 (approximately 10 minutes). Read the list on the left. Then write each item in an appropriate space on the right.

Topic: _____

dogs	Category 1: _____
Persian cats	Example _____
turtles	Example _____
other pets	Example _____
German shepherds	Example _____
birds	Category 2: _____
collies	Example _____
canaries	Example _____
white rats and gerbils	Example _____
Siamese cats	Example _____
monkeys	Category 3: _____
goldfish	Example _____
multi-colored average cats	Example _____
fish and reptiles	Example _____
snakes	Example _____
pets	Category 4: _____
black cats	Example _____
Siamese fighting fish	Example _____
parakeets	Example _____
cocker spaniels	Example _____
horses	Category 5: _____
poodles	Example _____
parrots	Example _____
cats	Example _____
	Example _____
	Example _____

The Whimbey Writing Program - Student Workbook 71

Exercise 2 (approximately 10 minutes). Notice that the classification outline on the right has two main categories, but one category has two subcategories. Write the items from the list on the left in the appropriate spaces on the right.

Topic: _____

Detroit	Category 1: _____
major U.S. cities	Subcategory A: _____
London	Example: _____
major northern U.S. cities	Example: _____
Tokyo	Example: _____
Chicago	Example: _____
Miami	Subcategory B: _____
Dallas	Example: _____
major cities of the world	Example: _____
major southern U.S. cities	Example: _____
Moscow	Example: _____
Paris	Category 2: _____
Atlanta	Example: _____
Houston	Example: _____
New York	Example: _____
Rome	Example: _____
Beijing	Example: _____
major foreign cities	Example: _____

Exercise 3 (approximately 15 minutes). For this exercise, notice that the classification outline has two main categories, but the first has two subcategories, whereas the second has three. Write the items from the list on the left in the appropriate spaces on the right.

Topic: _____

tables	Category 1: _____
dishwashers	Subcategory A: _____
furniture	Example: _____
merchandise sold in a store	Example: _____
merchandise for a home	Example: _____
silverware	Example: _____

dining merchandise
plates
washing machines
skirts
women's clothing
blouses
men's slacks
men's clothing
neckties
sofas
men's suits
clothing
appliances
desks
chairs
electric irons
drinking glasses

Subcategory B:_____
   Example:_____
   Example:_____
   Example:_____
   Example:_____
Category 2:_____
  Subcategory A:_____
   Example:_____
   Example:_____
   Example:_____
   Example:_____
  Subcategory B:_____
   Example:_____
   Example:_____
   Example:_____
   Example:_____
  Subcategory C:_____
   Example:_____
   Example:_____
   Example:_____
   Example:_____

Section 2
General-Specific

One of the most important techniques in effective writing is to give specific examples to support general statements. For example, if you are writing a paper arguing the general point that women are successfully entering traditionally male occupations, you might use women astronauts as a specific example. Moreover, in writing about women astronauts, you might use Sally Ride as a specific illustration, describing her experiences to make your ideas concrete. Of course, the terms general and specific are relative, as shown by this diagram.

- most general: <u>women successful in traditionally male occupations</u>
                         <u>women astronauts</u>

- most specific: <u>Sally Ride</u>

Forming general-specific relations is important in organizing many papers and is the focus of the following exercises. Try the sample exercise before reading the answer.

Sample Exercise. Write the following list in order, with the most general item on the top and the most specific on bottom.

List: American women   human beings   American women astronauts   Sally Ride   women

- most general: _____
- most specific: _____

Answer: Here is the best ordering.

- most general: human beings
                  women
                  American women
                  American women astronauts
- most specific: Sally Ride

This example shows that the idea of general-specific is closely related to classification. The term "human beings" includes both women and men, so human beings is more general than women. Moreover, the term "women" includes American women as well as non-American women, so women is more general than American women. Going one step further, the term "American women" includes American women astronauts as well as American women non-astronauts, so American women is more general than American women astronauts. The term "Sally Ride" is most specific because it refers to just one person. Now try the following exercises.

Exercises

Exercise 1 (approximately 5 minutes). Write each of the following sets of terms in the spaces provided, with the most general on top and the most specific on bottom.

List 1: tomato soups   foods   soups   liquid foods   Campbell's Tomato Soup

- most general: _____
- most specific: _____

74 *Organizing Ideas into Patterns*

List 2: furniture   metal chairs   manufactured objects   chairs   metal rocking chairs

- most general: _____
    _____
    _____
    _____
- most specific: _____

List 3: 27" stereo color television   communication appliances   color televisions   appliances

- most general: _____
    _____
    _____
    _____
- most specific: _____

List 4: successful professional athletes   successful athletes   successful professional quarterbacks   successful people   successful professional football players

- most general: _____
    _____
    _____
    _____
    _____
- most specific: _____

Exercise 2 (approximately 10 minutes). For each list, write something more general above the item already on the list, and something more specific below it.

List 1

- more general: _____
  ↓   _____meat_____
- more specific: _____

Here is a possible answer for list 1:

- more general: _____food_____
              _____meat_____
- more specific: _____beef_____

The term "food" includes meat as well as fruit, vegetables, and other edibles. So food is more general than meat. On the other hand, beef is one type of meat. So the term "beef" is more specific than meat. Use the same type of reasoning for the remaining exercises.

List 2

- more general: _____
  ↓   _____coats_____
- more specific: _____

List 3

- more general: _____
  ↓   ____professional singers____
- more specific: _____

List 4

- more general: _____
  ↓   _____doctors_____
- more specific: _____

List 5

- more general: _____
  ↓   _____cars_____
- more specific: _____

List 6

- more general: _____
  ↓   _____magazines_____
- more specific: _____

List 7

- more general: _____
  ↓   ___human-powered vehicles___
- more specific: _____

Section 3
Analysis of Organizing Ideas

This chapter introduced two patterns for arranging ideas: classification and general-specific. You may have noticed a relationship between the patterns. A classification has a topic and categories. The topic is general and each category is more specific. This relationship between the patterns is shown on the diagram:

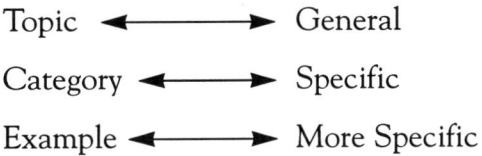

Although the two patterns are related, they are used in different situations. When you are describing a set of things (like popular pets), you might classify them into categories and write a classification paper. But when you are writing a paper to prove the truth of a general statement, you try to think of two or three specific examples that support your statement and then present these examples with even more specific details. For example, in writing a paper entitled "Pets Are Useful to People," you would not write a classification paper on all pets. Instead, you would describe a few specific examples like German shepherds working as seeing-eye dogs and monkeys being trained to aid persons with limited mobility. Furthermore, to make your points clear and convincing, your paper would need specific details like how seeing-eye dogs help a blind person avoid obstacles and cross streets. You might even be more specific and describe a trip to the store by a blind man with his dog. Classification papers are illustrated in the next chapter, whereas papers presenting general statements supported by specific details are covered in Chapters 6, 7, and 8.

Answer to Sample Exercise on p. 70

<u>Transportation vehicles</u> is the broadest term in the list. It includes land transportation vehicles, water transportation vehicles, and air transportation vehicles. So transportation vehicles belongs in the space labeled "Topic." The three categories are land transportation vehicles, water transportation vehicles, and air transportation vehicles. These could be written in any order in the spaces labeled "Category 1, 2, and 3." The examples are then listed within the categories. In the answer, the first two categories begin with examples of motorized vehicles and then list non-motorized vehicles because this is how you might discuss them in a paper—moving from motorized to non-motorized. The third category has no non-motorized vehicles because none is widely used for air transportation. (You might have added gliders and hot air balloons if you wanted to discuss them in a paper.)

Topic: transportation vehicles
    Category 1:   land transportation vehicles
        Example: automobiles
        Example: motorcycles
        Example: trucks
        Example: buses
        Example: trains
        Example: bicycles
    Category 2:   water transportation vehicles
        Example: ocean liners
        Example: motorboats and motorized yachts
        Example: submarines
        Example: sailboats
        Example: canoes
        Example:
    Category 3:   air transportation vehicles
        Example: jet passenger planes
        Example: helicopters
        Example: small private planes
        Example: spacecraft
        Example:
        Example:

Chapter 5
Classification

This chapter provides more experience in classification. One of the ways people make sense of the world is to classify things into groups on the basis of similarities and differences. Potatoes, cabbages, spinach, and other edible roots and leafy plants are classified together as vegetables, whereas sweeter, seed-bearing plants like cherries, apples, and pears are placed in a separate class called "fruits." Another example is the classified telephone directory (the "Yellow Pages"), where businesses are classified alphabetically by type: Accountants, Advertising Agencies, Automobile Dealers, etc. Because we think in terms of classifications, much of our writing reflects this organizational pattern.

Classification papers often include three to five categories of persons, things, actions, or ideas. Generally, two or three characteristics are focused on describing the distinctive features of each category. For instance, one of the exercises in this chapter concerns the branches of the United States government. Each branch is described in terms of three characteristics: type of activities, parts or divisions, and method for selecting officials. A paper written with this classification pattern would have the following outline:

Topic: Branches of the U.S. Government

    Category 1. Executive Branch
        type of activities
        parts or divisions
        officials

Category 2. Legislative Branch
   type of activities
   parts or divisions
   officials

Category 3. Judicial Branch
   type of activities
   parts or divisions
   officials

Some classification papers are more complicated and include subcategories within the main categories, as you will see in Section 4's discussion about varieties of cheese.

The wide range of topics lending themselves to the classification pattern is shown in the exercises that follow. Some classifications, like the branches of government, were created intentionally by people. Others, such as the varieties of cheese, evolved gradually over time and somewhat haphazardly. Finally, classifications like the "types of campers" in Section 5 are caricatures, created as much to amuse as describe. Working through the exercises will strengthen your ability to write informative sentences tied together into a well-organized classification paper.

Section 1
Grades of Beef

The following sentences can be organized into a paragraph on the categories used for different grades of beef.

Exercises

Exercise 1 (approximately 5 minutes). Number the sentences to form a paragraph that begins with a question to arouse the reader's interest.

____ It comes from young, well-fed animals and has lines of fat running throughout the meat, making it juicy and tender.

____ Although not as tender, they can provide healthy, low-budget meals.

____ The best quality beef is labeled Prime.

____ Choice is the second highest quality.

___ When shopping for beef at the supermarket, have you ever wondered about the difference between cuts labeled "Prime" and those called "Choice" or "Good?"

___ But Good beef can be made tender and delicious by cooking it properly.

___ There are several grades of meat below these three.

___ Beef labeled Good has little fat and is less tender than the two better grades.

___ Choice has less fat than Prime but is still juicy and tender.

___ They are also used for ground beef and popular meat products like the hot dog.

Exercise 2 (approximately 5 minutes). Write the sentences in the order you numbered them to form a classification paragraph for grades of beef.

_____
_____
_____
_____
_____
_____
_____
_____
_____
_____
_____
_____
_____

Section 2
My Car, the Image

What's in a name? Do you buy products because of their names? The following sentences can be arranged into a brief classification paper taking a critical look at product name as a sales and marketing tactic.

Exercises

Exercise 1 (approximately 10 minutes). Number the sentences within each paragraph in the best logical order. For paragraphs 2, 3, and 4, first present the type of car name, then some examples, and finally the analysis of why such names are appealing.

First Paragraph

____ They vary in size, performance characteristics, price, image, and fuel economy—all to be considered when purchasing a car.

____ Automobiles are a major part of modern American life, and most families own at least one.

____ However, manufacturers often give names to cars that suggest exciting or desirable characteristics which appeal to our emotions, but can cloud our thinking.

____ Obviously, the name of a car does not affect how it drives.

Second Paragraph

____ Such names suggest the power and speed of wild, uninhibited beasts in nature.

____ An old but still common trick is to christen automobiles with the names of real or mythical animals.
(*Vocabulary Tips: christen*– to name; *mythical*– not real, from a myth.)

____ Through the years we have seen Hudson's Hornet, Buick's Wild Cat, Mercury's Cougar, Ford's Mustang and Thunderbird, and Leyland's Jaguar.

Third Paragraph

____ The Buick Riviera, Cadillac Seville, and Chrysler New Yorker fit into this category.
(*Vocabulary Tip: Riviera*– section of southern Europe with beautiful beaches and rich, glamorous people.)

___ Another ploy of car makers is to borrow names from pleasant or elegant places.
(*Vocabulary Tip: ploy– trick.*)

___ Supposedly, stepping into these vehicles transports you from your dull hometown to the haunts of the rich and glamorous.
(*Vocabulary Tip: transport– move from one place to another*).

Fourth Paragraph

___ They also suggest associations with racing cars, which generally have large numbers or letters painted on them.

___ These designations give the impression of high-tech mechanical performance.

___ Examples are the Chevrolet Z28, Mazda MX6, Saab 9000CD, and all the GT, LX, and EX models.

___ The most recent trend has been to use numbers or letters as names.

Fifth Paragraph

___ Pick a car for its performance and design qualities, not for the connotations of its name.

___ As an intelligent car buyer, guard against being fooled by such glamorous names and labels.

Exercise 2 (approximately 10 minutes). Write the sentences into a paper about three categories of names that manufacturers use to sell cars.

_____

_____

_____

_____

_____

_____

_____

_____

Exercise 3 (approximately 25 minutes). With all material from the preceding exercises put away, write a brief (150 words) classification paper on the suggestive power of automobile names. You may use any ideas or language that you remember from the paper or draw upon your own experiences.

Section 3
Classification System for the U.S. Government

Can you write a description of the classification system underlying the activities of your government? The following sentences can be arranged into a thumbnail sketch of the U.S. government.

Exercises

Exercise 1 (approximately 10 minutes). Number the sentences within each paragraph to form the best logical order. Describe each government branch (paragraphs 2, 3, 4) in terms of type of activities, divisions or departments, and officials.

First Paragraph

____ So they divided the activities of our government among three branches, preventing any single person or group from becoming too powerful.

____ The writers of our constitution wanted to insure that the U.S. would be free from what they considered to be the tyranny of kings prevailing in Europe at the time.
(Vocabulary Tips: prevailing– dominating, occurring most frequently; tyranny– government where one ruler wields total power, often selfishly or cruelly.)

____ The three branches, created and empowered by the Constitution, are the Executive, Legislative, and Judicial.
(Vocabulary Tip: empowered– given power.)

Second Paragraph

____ To perform these duties the Executive branch includes the Defense Department, with the Army, Navy, Air Force, and Marines; the Treasury Department, with the IRS, Customs Service, and Bureau of Engraving and Printing; the Justice Department (FBI); the Transportation Department; and many other agencies.

____ The President is the chief of this branch, hiring or firing the department heads, and is selected every four years in an election open to all adult citizens.

____ The Executive branch executes the country's laws and protects it during war.
(Vocabulary tip: executes– carries out.)

Third Paragraph

___ Each state elects two senators who represent it for six-year terms, but the number of representatives (with two-year terms) it sends to the House depends on its population: more population, more representation.

___ This branch consists of the Senate and the House of Representatives, together called the Congress.

___ Both the Senate and the House have many committees, such as the Finance Committee and the Foreign Relations Committee, which study issues and make recommendations on new laws, taxes, and national spending.
(*Vocabulary Tip: issues– controversies, topics under discussion.*)

___ The Legislative branch makes laws for the country and holds the "power of the purse"— the authority to levy taxes and decide how the money is spent.

Fourth Paragraph

___ Such judgments are needed when two people (or groups) differ in their interpretation of the law, or when the law has been broken and a judgment must be made about the appropriate punishment.

___ The Judicial branch interprets and makes judgments about the law.

___ Federal judges are appointed by the President and must be approved by the Senate.

___ The appointments are for life, which helps free judges from political pressure.

___ The work of this branch is done by district courts, appeals courts, and the Supreme Court.

___ Most cases start in district courts.

___ If she is still dissatisfied, she may try to take her case to the Supreme Court.

___ If a person disagrees with the judgment of a district courts, she can go to an appeals court and have the case judged again.

___ The Supreme Court, which handles cases of great national importance, has the final authority in legal judgments and also the power to decide whether any new law violates the Constitution and must be changed or abolished.

Fifth Paragraph

___ The proof is that for over 200 years the three branches have kept each other from assuming excessive power while working together for the benefit of the nation.

___ Dividing the activities of our government among three branches has functioned as the writers of our Constitution hoped it would.

Exercise 2 (approximately 15 minutes). Write the sentences in the order you numbered them to form a classification paper on the U.S. government.

Section 4
A Cheese for All Tastes

Can you use classification to write a paper on the "humble" subject of cheese?

Exercises

Exercise 1 (approximately 3 minutes). Number the following sentences to form an introductory first paragraph that:

- first arouses a reader's appetite and interest in cheese;

- then provides a little background information; and

- finally introduces a classification of cheeses.

First Paragraph

____ Over the years, so many varieties have been developed that a person is almost sure to find one type appealing to the tastebuds.

____ In fact, cheese is one of man's oldest foods, mentioned even in the *Old Testament* of the *Bible*.

____ Pizza, cheeseburgers, cheese fondue, and cheese Danish are just some of the delectable foods we would miss without cheese.

____ The assorted cheeses you can buy in supermarkets and cheese stores fall into two categories, natural cheese and processed cheese; furthermore, natural cheese may be either unripened or ripened.

Exercise 2 (approximately 12 minutes). Now, number the sentences in each of the five following paragraphs to form a paper that continues the cheese classification just introduced.

Second Paragraph

____ The whey is partially drained, and the curd is refined into unripened cheese.

____ Rennet causes the solid material of milk to form into white lumps called curd, leaving just a thin liquid known as whey.

___ Cottage cheese, made from skim milk, is an important food for dieters because it is rich in protein and other nutrients but low in calories.

___ Three common unripened cheeses are Cottage, Ricotta, and Cream.

___ Ricotta cheese, made from whole milk, is smoother than Cottage cheese and is used in tasty Italian dishes like lasagna.

___ The simplest cheese, unripened natural cheese, is made by adding rennet (derived from calf stomach enzyme) to milk.

___ It is used in sandwiches and in baking the popular dessert, cheesecake.

___ Cream cheese is the richest of the three because it is made from cream.

Third Paragraph

___ By contrast, ripened cheeses are more flavorful because they go through an additional step in production.

___ The unripened cheeses described above have mild flavors, as you probably know from tasting them.

___ This is called ripening, and different cultures are used to give various cheeses their distinctive flavors and textures.

_5_ Ripened cheeses are labeled mild, medium, or sharp indicating the length of time they were ripened.

___ Limburger, for example, is so soft it can be spread on crackers, Swiss is firm and usually sliced, while Parmesan is so hard it must be grated and sprinkled on food.

___ Ripened cheeses also vary in softness, determined mainly by moisture content.

___ The sharpest cheeses are produced through long ripening and may be labeled aged.

___ In addition, blue cheese and Roquefort are veined with blue streaks produced by the cultures used for ripening.

_3_ Cultures (small living organisms) are added to the cheese and allowed to grow.

___ Regarding color, ripened cheeses range from the white of Brick to the golden yellow of aged Cheddar.

Fourth Paragraph

___ Emulsifiers make cheese blend smoothly, slice easily, and melt readily.

___ Other processed cheeses acquire their flavor from different natural cheeses and added ingredients like bacon or hickory smoke.

___ Besides the variety of natural cheeses just described, cheese merchants have provided customers with even more choices by creating processed cheese.

___ One popular processed cheese is American cheese, which has the natural cheese called Cheddar as its main ingredient.

___ Processed cheese is manufactured by grinding, heating, and mixing natural cheeses with emulsifiers.

Fifth Paragraph

___ A variation of processed cheese has been given the name processed cheese food.

___ The milk also produces a milder flavor, which some people prefer to the strong flavor of natural cheese.

___ Processed cheese food is mixed like processed cheese, but milk or whey is added to make it softer and easier to spread.

___ The appeal of cold pack is not its ease in spreading but the delicious flavors created by blending fine, aged cheeses.

___ Another variation of processed cheese, called "cold pack" is made by mixing well-aged natural cheeses without adding much moisture or emulsifiers.

Sixth Paragraph

___ This provides an easy way to discover new, tasty cheeses that you can add to your menu in appetizers, sandwiches, and sauces, making one of life's basic pleasures, eating, even more pleasurable.

___ Most cities have cheese stores that offer bite-sized free samples of numerous cheeses to help customers in their selection.

Exercise 3 (approximately 15 minutes). Write the sentences in the order you numbered them to form a classification paper on cheese.

Exercise 4 (approximately 10 minutes). In the last chapter you arranged ideas into a classification pattern. The cheese paper basically has that pattern, although one of the categories (processed cheese) doesn't have subcategories but rather one example and two variations. Fill the blanks in the following outline for the cheese paper. Note: For <u>Examples</u> list specific cheeses like Cheddar, not qualities like "soft."

Topic: _____

  Category 1: _____

    Subcategory: _____

      Example: _____

      Example: _____

      Example: _____

    Subcategory: _____

      Example: _____

      Example: _____

      Example: _____

      Example: _____

      Example: _____

  Category 2: _____

    Example: _____

      Variation: _____

      Variation: _____

Section 5
Not All Campers Camp

The following sentences can be arranged into a humorous classification paper on campers.

Exercises

Exercise 1 (approximately 10 minutes). Number the sentences so they are logically ordered within each paragraph. If several arrangements are possible for a paragraph, pick the one you like best.

First Paragraph

___ This quest for travel-adventure-on-a-budget has greatly swelled the population of campers.

___ And by spending a few nights at a campground, local or distant, one discovers there are three major types who seek such temporary habitation: those who sleep away from their vehicles (campers); those who "plan" to sleep away from their vehicles (pseudocampers); and those who sleep in their vehicles (RV'ers).
(*Vocabulary Tip: habitation– residence, place where one lives.*)

___ Americans have taken to the roads in a big way lately.

___ They are seeking new horizons, exploring historical spots once only read about, and visiting the latest tourist attractions yet trying to avoid expensive airline fares and motel rates.

Second Paragraph

_4_ Their equipment is often expensive, but it is designed for years of use by people who prefer to face the elements of nature wherever they can—even if only at a KOA campground.

___ When compared to motel motorists, jet-setting hotelers, or even RV'ers, the campers are not just bargain hunters but true lovers of camping.

___ These modern day Daniel Boones are independent and self-sufficient.

___ They enjoy chopping wood and cooking over an open fire and ignore the available electricity.

___ These hearty souls realize the existing dangers (hungry animals, poisonous snakes, accidents)—but brave it all just to truly camp.

___ Some in this group are so ardent that they avoid the campgrounds of the masses and look for places in the actual wilderness to pitch their tents.

Third Paragraph

___ For weeks, their neighbors listen to their plans to camp during the upcoming vacation.

___ The car is loaded with the tent and other camping gear in anticipation of the adventure to come.

___ A necessary part for pitching the tent has been forgotten; the weather is too hot (or too cold or too damp); or they find a motel room almost as cheap as the campground (and because they are really only camping to save money, it would be silly not to stay at the motel, even if the pool is tiny and overcrowded).

___ However, there usually is something to prevent them from actually camping.

___ Never-used or just sampled, the tent ends up in the trunk of the car until it becomes a mildew farm.

___ Next are the pseudo-campers.

___ Sometimes these people do use their tents for a night or two, but they invariably decide that they simply do not enjoy camping.

Fourth Paragraph

___ Although it does cost a few extra dollars for the availability of electricity to use today's most modern conveniences, the RV'ers do not complain.

___ They are not really bargain hunters.

___ Finally, there are the RV'ers, who sleep in their vehicles on the other side of the campground from the true campers, in the "full hook-up" section.

___ After all, some recreational vehicles cost as much as or more than a small house—so what's a few more dollars?

___ The high vehicle price and the estimated "dollar-a-mile" to make it run may explain why so many RV'ers seldom spend time away from their vehicles on vacations.

___ Forget about nature; they've brought their home with them.

___ An early evening tour of their section of the campground proves that most of them are "home:" the air conditioners are running full blast, and the TVs are blaring their favorite programs, while the steaks simmer in the microwaves.

Fifth Paragraph

___ However, regardless of which type one is, camping offers the chance to trade everyday activities for new experiences away from home.

___ Personal preference for conveniences, money, and the amount of daring one possesses usually are the deciding factors determining the type of camper one chooses to be.

Exercise 2 (approximately 15 minutes). Write the sentences in the order you numbered them to form a classification paper on campers.

Section 6
Analysis of Classification Papers

The exercises in this unit illustrated classification paragraphs and papers. In starting your own classification papers, avoid the common error of choosing a topic that is too broad for the amount of writing you plan to do. For example, the car image paper begins with these two sentences:

> Automobiles are a major part of modern American life. They vary in size, performance characteristics, price, fuel economy, and image—all to be considered when purchasing one.

These two sentences introduce a topic that is too broad for the short paper that follows. In 250 words it is not possible to classify and describe automobiles in terms of size, performance, price, economy, and image. Such a paper would require at least 1,000 words to even briefly cover the necessary facts and examples. Always choose a topic that you can cover with sufficient detail in the length of paper you plan to write. Then formulate your opening sentences so they reflect exactly what the rest of the paper discusses. If your opening sentences promise more than your paper delivers, your readers will be unimpressed with you as either a writer or a solid thinker. The opening paragraph of the car image paper narrows the topic with its second pair of sentences:

> Obviously the name of a car does not affect how it drives. But manufacturers often give names to cars which suggest exciting or desirable characteristics that appeal to our emotions and so cloud our thinking.

The last sentence serves as a transition or bridge between the general topic of automobiles and the specific focus of the rest of the paper. In addition to introducing the topic of a paper, a good opening may try to arouse a reader's interest. One common technique for snagging the reader's attention is to ask a question, such as: When shopping for beef at the supermarket, have you ever wondered about the difference between cuts labeled "Prime" and those called "Choice" or "Good?" If you ask the right question, a person will read further to find the answer.

Another technique is to excite the senses with a vivid, concrete description like: Pizza, cheeseburgers, cheese fondue, and cheese Danish—just some of the delectable foods we would miss without cheese.

The last function that the introduction may serve is to provide a little background information on the topic, such as:

> Americans have taken to the roads in a big way lately. They are seeking new horizons, exploring historical spots once only read about, and visiting the latest tourist attractions yet trying to avoid expensive airline fares and motel rates. This quest for travel-adventure-on-a-budget has greatly swelled the population of campers.

After the introduction, you begin to describe the categories. One way is with openings like these:

    One type of . . . .   The first kind of . . . .   The cheapest category of . . . .

    The second group of . . . .   The next type is . . . .   Another kind of . . . .

    Turning to the next category . . . .   The last category is . . . .   The final type is . . . . .

Another method for introducing a new category is through comparison with a previous category, such as: Beef labeled "Good" is less tender than the two higher grades.

But such beginnings are not always necessary. Often, just starting a new paragraph signifies a new category, and you can simply name and begin describing it with a sentence like: The legislative branch of the government was empowered by the Constitution to make new laws for the country.

In describing the distinctive features for each category, try to present the details in parallel (the same order) whenever possible. In the car images paper, each paragraph could be arranged to begin with the general statement about the type of car name, then present several examples, and finally explain the appeal of the category. If you changed this order for different paragraphs, the paper might appear confused and disorganized.

In some cases, a completely parallel description of all the details in each category may not be appropriate. You may emphasize different details in different categories according to their significance. In the cheese paper, distinctive flavors were emphasized in describing ripened cheeses, but practicality for spreading and cooking was highlighted for processed cheese. Ripened cheese is valued for flavor, processed cheese for practicality. Generally, however, you will have the same two or three characteristics in mind as you describe all the categories. When your subject lends itself to parallel description of these characteristics, certainly use it for the clarity it adds to communication.

Whenever possible, try to write a conclusion that draws your paper together. This is how the cheese paper was summed up:

> Most cities have cheese stores that offer bite-sized free samples of numerous cheeses to help customers in their selection. This provides an easy way to discover new, tasty cheeses that you can add to your menu in appetizers, sandwiches, and sauces, making one of life's basic pleasures, eating, even more pleasurable.

This conclusion has a positive tone because the entire paper was positive about cheese. Of course, for a paper taking a critical or negative view of the categories, the conclusion would summarize that position, as in the car images paper:

> As an intelligent car buyer, guard against being fooled by such glamorous names and labels. Pick a car for its performance and design qualities, not for the connotations of its name.

Both of these endings illustrate that an effective way to close a classification paper is with a general observation about the whole array of things categorized. One more example is seen in the campers paper, which ended:

> ... regardless of which type one is, camping offers the chance to trade everyday activities for new experiences away from home.

Section 7
Independent Writing

In doing the following assignments, remember that good writers generally read through and revise a paper TWO or THREE times before considering it finished. After you write a first draft, read it from the beginning and revise sentences that can be expressed more clearly or smoothly. Also add any new ideas and examples that you think are important, REWRITING THE WHOLE PAPER IF NECESSARY. Finally, read your paper once more to catch spelling and grammar errors.

Exercises

Exercise 1 (approximately 30 minutes). Food may be categorized as meat (including seafood), dairy (milk, cheese, yogurt), grains (bread, noodles, cereal), and produce (vegetables, fruits). Write a classification paper (about 500 words) on these four categories of food. If there are important subcategories within the four broad categories, include them in the paper. Describe each category systematically. For each category you might first give examples of that type of food, then explain how the food is obtained, and finally describe how it is prepared and eaten. You will probably find it useful to first make an outline, grouping foods into categories and listing ideas you will write about for each category.

If you have trouble thinking of ideas, try brainstorming for three minutes. You could write down every idea about food that comes into your mind. Or you could begin with meat, writing down every idea about meat that comes to mind: kinds of meat, how you cook them, etc. Then brainstorm for each of the other categories. After brainstorming, organize the ideas into a category-by-category outline. At the same time, try to think of sentences to introduce and explain the ideas for each category. Talk to yourself as if you were describing foods to someone else. Write down any useful ideas, sentences, or paragraphs because this will make your job of writing the paper easier. Then write a first draft of the paper, read it critically, and revise it to correct spelling or grammar errors and to express and illustrate your ideas more clearly.

Exercise 2 (approximately 20 minutes). Write a classification paper on vehicles that travel the streets. For each category, present a physical description of each vehicle, its major use, and other relevant information.

Exercise 3 (approximately 20 minutes). Write a classification paper on TV shows. For each category in your paper, describe examples of specific shows and also the appeal or effect on the audience for that type of show.

You might begin by brainstorming. Take one minute to list all the shows and types of shows that you can. It might help to think of shows broadcast in the morning, in the afternoon, at dinner time, on a specific night, etc.

Exercise 4 (approximately 30 minutes). Think of three types of people, such as three types of drivers, students, athletes, dressers, or dancers. Then make up names for the three types. For dressers these might be "GQ boy," "slob," and "straight." Next, brainstorm ideas to describe their appearance, actions, or other distinguishing characteristics. Include plenty of details so your readers can actually "see" the three types. Organize the ideas into an outline, including any sentences that you think of to introduce and express your ideas. Finally, write a classification paper on the three types, as was illustrated in the campers paper.

Chapter 6
Generalization Supported by Specific Details

A generalization is a broad statement such as "San Diego is a great place to live," or "My childhood prepared me well for adult life." To convince people that a generalization is correct, you must give them specific details that support or illustrate it. What makes San Diego a great place to live? The climate? The geography? The business or recreational opportunities? Specific details make your writing persuasive, interesting, and easier to understand.

Remember from Chapter 4 that the terms general and specific are relative, as shown in the diagram.

- more general   increases in the cost of living
-   ↓   increases in the cost of entertainment
- more specific   increase in the cost of going to a movie

A paper might begin with this generalization: There has been a sharp increase in the cost of living over the past ten years. Then each paragraph could describe a specific increase, such as the increase in entertainment, housing, or transportation costs. Within the paragraph on entertainment costs the writer could present illustrations that are even more specific, such as increases in admission fees and food at the movie theater. The overall paper would have this form:

      Paragraph 1.   Generalization   There has been a sharp increase in the cost of living over the past ten years, as seen by the rise in entertainment, housing, and transportation costs.

Paragraph 2.	Support A	Entertainment expenses have increased. Examples: admission and popcorn prices.
Paragraph 3.	Support B	Housing costs have increased. Examples: buying, renting, and heating costs
Paragraph 4.	Support C	Transportation costs have increased. Examples: car purchase, repair, and fuel prices
Paragraph 5.	Conclusion	Generalization restated and ideas summarized.

The following exercises begin with illustrations of how individual paragraphs are made interesting and convincing by including specific details to support generalizations. The exercises then progress to three- and four-paragraph selections and eventually an eight-paragraph paper, all with the generalization-specifics pattern. The topics range from personal concerns, such as choosing a pet, to public issues like false advertising or the location of a city's convention center.

Section 1
You Can't Afford to be Sick

A generalization is a broad statement. Here is an example of a generalization.

- Hospital costs have skyrocketed since the 1970s.

When you state a generalization, you usually need one or more examples to make the generalization clear and convincing, as illustrated in the exercise below.

Exercises

Exercise 1 (approximately 5 minutes). Number the following sentences to form a paragraph that begins with a generalization and then supports it with examples. One sentence has already been given the number 4.

____ For example, in 1975 a bed in a semi-private room at Boston Memorial was $95 a day.

____ Now the bill for the same room is $200 a day.

____ Hospital costs have skyrocketed since the 1970s.

_4_   It has even become unbearably expensive to bear children.
(Vocabulary Tips: unbearable– too painful or difficult to withstand; bear– give birth to.)

___   But last week, 7 lb. Billy Wilson cost his parents $900 to be born there, about $130 a pound.

___   Manhattan General Hospital charged $400 for a normal delivery in 1975 (not counting the physician's fee).
(Vocabulary Tip: delivery– birth of a baby.)

___   Again, this did not include the physician's fee, which also more than doubled in size during the period.

Exercise 2 (approximately 10 minutes). Write the sentences in the order you numbered them to form a paragraph supporting the generalization that hospital costs have skyrocketed.

_____

_____

_____

_____

_____

_____

_____

_____

_____

_____

_____

_____

_____

_____

_____

Section 2
Pick Good Supporting Evidence

In writing a convincing generalization-specifics paper, it is important to include specifics that actually support your generalization. Ideas that are only loosely associated with the generalization may sometimes be worked into the paper to arouse interest and to provide background information, but the weight of your argument must be carried by direct supporting evidence.

Exercises

Exercise 1 (approximately 5 minutes). Only four of the following eight sentences support the statement: Trees provide us with many benefits. Write those four sentences in the space provided. You may write the four sentences in any order.

- We must be careful to control forest fires because it takes years for trees to grow back in a burned area.

- Apples, pears, and many other fruits come from trees.

- Among the largest and oldest living things in the world are the California Redwoods, some of which stand over 300 feet tall and have been growing since the days of the ancient Greeks.

- Huge quantities of lumber from trees are used by the home construction and furniture industries.

- If we don't plant new trees to replace the ones we cut down, our children won't have any.

- When the pilgrims came to America, there were trees stretching from the east coast to the west coast, except for some plains and desert areas.

- The shade of a tree can be a great comfort on a hot summer day.

- Trees absorb carbon dioxide and give out oxygen, which humans need to breathe.

Trees provide us with many benefits.

1. _____

2. _____

3. _____

4. _____

Exercise 2 (approximately 5 minutes). From the remaining sentences, write two that could be used in discussing the history of trees.

1. _____

2. _____

Exercise 3 (approximately 5 minutes). Write the two sentences dealing most directly with the conservation (saving and protection) of trees.

1. _____

2. _____

Section 3
The Wonderful Plastic Card

Exercises

Exercise 1 (approximately 10 minutes). The following sentences include a general statement about credit cards and supporting examples. Number the sentences within each paragraph to form the best logical order.

First Paragraph

___ You can go to a department store and pick out a giant-screen TV, stereo system, or warm winter coat, then enjoy your purchase while paying for it over time.

___ At home it increases your buying power for large, expensive items.

___ A credit card is an extremely useful little piece of plastic, both at home and on a trip.

Second Paragraph

___ Cash or traveler's cheques won't satisfy them.

___ On a trip the card permits you to purchase meals, lodging, gas, and souvenirs without carrying a wallet stuffed full of $20 and $50 bills.

___ But the piece of plastic identifies you as a responsible person with some financial stability, a person to be trusted with one of their vehicles.
(Vocabulary Tip: stability– lack of change, reliability, permanence.)

___ In fact, if you try to rent a car during your trip, you'll find you won't be able to get one from any of the major auto rental agencies without a credit card.

Third Paragraph

___ Moreover, as soon as you report the card stolen to a 24-hour telephone number, your financial responsibility ceases.
(Vocabulary Tips: moreover– furthermore, in addition; ceases– ends.)

___ Generally, there is a $50 limit on your responsibility for someone else's illegal use of your card.

___ In short, a credit card gives you all the purchasing power of continually carrying several hundred dollars, but none of the risk.
(Vocabulary Tip: in short– in summary, all in all.)

___ Perhaps most important, whether you are at home or traveling, you don't have to worry about your credit card getting lost or stolen, the way loose cash can cause worry.

Exercise 2 (approximately 10 minutes). Write the preceding sentences in the order you numbered them.

_____

_____

_____

_____

_____

_____

_____

_____

_____

Exercise 3 (OPTIONAL, approximately 20 minutes). With all of the preceding materials out of sight, write a short paper arguing why credit cards are (or are not) very useful.

Section 4
The Family Needs a New Truck

When you recommend an expensive purchase like buying a new truck, you need convincing reasons with specific facts to win your case. The following sentences can be arranged to make a well-supported argument for a new truck that you would like to drive.

Exercises

Exercise 1 (approximately 10 minutes). Number the sentences within each paragraph to form the best logical order.

First Paragraph

____ Nevertheless, we should buy a new truck because the old truck is unreliable, obtaining parts for it is difficult, and the greater economy of a new truck would help repay the purchase price.

____ It is true that new trucks are expensive, and the family's budget is tight.

Second Paragraph

____ Worse yet, last Friday it quit running on the expressway and had to be towed to a garage.

____ Three times last month dad was late to work because the truck would not start.

____ Dad is sure to get in trouble with his boss if this continues.

____ The old truck is constantly breaking down.

Third Paragraph

____ This means they have to special-order the parts, which usually takes several hours and once took two days.

____ Another problem is getting replacement parts.

____ Because of its age, most repair shops don't stock the hoses, belts, mufflers, or other parts it requires.

Fourth Paragraph

___ Our old clunker only gets about 12 miles per gallon on the highway and less in the city.

___ Not only are there the savings on repair costs, but we can choose a truck that gets much better gas mileage.

___ Looking at the brighter side, a new truck would eventually pay for itself.

___ All things considered, buying a new truck makes a lot of sense.

___ Some of the newer models average as much as 30 or 40 miles per gallon.

Exercise 2 (approximately 15 minutes). Write the sentences in the order you numbered them to form a short paper which expresses an opinion that a certain action should be taken and supports that opinion with three specific reasons (including examples).

_____
_____
_____
_____
_____
_____
_____
_____
_____
_____

Section 5
The Perfect Pet

What is the perfect pet? The following sentences present one opinion along with supporting details.

Exercises

Exercise 1 (approximately 15 minutes). Number the sentences within each paragraph to form the best logical order.

First Paragraph

___ When you add that it is odorless, quiet, and a super traveling companion, you will begin to understand my partiality for this creature.
(Vocabulary Tip: partiality– preference, liking for something.)

___ This feisty little crustacean is inexpensive to buy and keep and does not have to be housebroken.
(Vocabulary Tips: feisty– quarrelsome, full of nervous energy; crustacean– shellfish, like a crab.)

___ If you are thinking about acquiring a new pet, let me suggest that you consider a hermit crab.

Second Paragraph

___ Most pets cost much more, and their purchase price is just the beginning of an expensive relationship.

___ Being in the right pet store at the right time (because hermit crabs are sometimes difficult to find) is all you must do to get one of these pets for less than $5.

___ The average pet, especially a furry one, requires regular veterinarian visits for shots to prevent rabies and distemper, treatment of various illnesses and accidents, and medicines to fight heart worms, stomach worms, ticks, and fleas.

___ Fish owners must first buy an elaborate tank system and then spend more money maintaining the delicate balances of temperature and water chemistry that are required within this domicile.
(*Vocabulary Tip: domicile– home, place where one lives.*)

___ Finny friends stay out of the doctor's office, but their housing costs are high and can easily become astronomical.
(*Vocabulary Tip: astronomical– very large.*)

Third Paragraph

___ With a little imagination you can make its habitat from leftovers and inexpensive materials.
(*Vocabulary Tip: habitat– home or home territory.*)

___ A hermit crab, on the other hand, neither sees a doctor nor demands a costly, elaborate home.

___ Add a few twigs for climbing, a shallow dish for water, and some kitty litter, cedar shavings, or shredded newspaper for a hiding place, and this pet is practically "home free."

___ A recycled leaky fish tank will make an excellent cage.

Fourth Paragraph

___ Just the elimination of this housekeeping routine makes it an ideal pet as far as I'm concerned.

___ Because a hermit crab is such a light eater, its body wastes are so minimal that its cage only needs to be cleaned every two months.

116   Generalization Supported by Specific Details

___ You never have to rush home from school to take it out for a walk so it can eliminate its wastes in front of someone else's house instead of in yours.

___ You also completely avoid the tasks of teaching it to use a newspaper and cleaning up when it doesn't.

Fifth Paragraph

___ Other pets can cause large odor problems.

___ Another charming attribute of a hermit crab is that it is odor-free.

_3_ Most pet owners who have a dog, cat, or other four-legged or winged animal have discovered that the amount of effort needed to avoid unpleasant and lingering pet odors grows in direct proportion to the animal's size.

_5_ You may not notice the change in the air around you, but others will.

___ And if your house is indeed your pet's house, no amount of care can assure that a foul smell won't spread throughout your home as the pet roams about while you are away.

Sixth Paragraph

___ But a hermit crab is always a silent partner.

___ Other people may also be annoyed by the various sounds pets make.

___ To me there is nothing more irritating than a dog that barks at anything that moves or a cat that howls at other cats as they prepare to fight or romance each other.

Seventh Paragraph

___ Of course, you could leave yours at home because it can easily survive for two weeks without care (providing it has enough water and food in its cage).

___ Because hermit crabs are so quiet, they also make super traveling companions.

_3_ However, should you elect to take your hermit along, no special travel arrangements will be needed.

___ "No Pets" signs may be ignored with total confidence.

___ Your pocket or palm makes a perfect traveling compartment wherever you roam.

_6_ No one will ever know you are traveling with your pet unless you volunteer a peek.

___ And one doggie bag could keep it well fed for years.

___ Even dining on the road is not a problem because your hermit crab can get by the most scrutinizing hostess or maitre d'.
(*Vocabulary Tip: scrutinizing– examining closely and critically.*)

Eighth Paragraph

___ Those nifty creatures sell very quickly because the public is beginning to realize what a unique and undemanding friend a hermit can be.

___ If you would like to know more about hermit crabs as pets, the best way is to try sharing your life with one.

___ I suggest that you call a pet store and request that one or two hermits be saved for you when the next shipment arrives.

Exercise 2 (approximately 15 minutes). Write the sentences in the order you numbered them to form a paper arguing that hermit crabs are great pets.

_____

_____

_____

_____

_____

_____

_____

_____

_____

_____

_____

_____

Exercise 3 (**OPTIONAL**, approximately 30 minutes). Write a paper (minimum 150 words) about the animal you would like most for a pet and why. If the animal is a hermit crab, make sure all materials from exercises 1 and 2 are away. If you would not want to own any pet, write a paper explaining your reasons.

Section 6
Ordering Supporting Details

When you present several specific examples to support a statement, you may order them from least to most impressive so that your argument ends on a strong point. This is illustrated in the first exercise.

Exercises

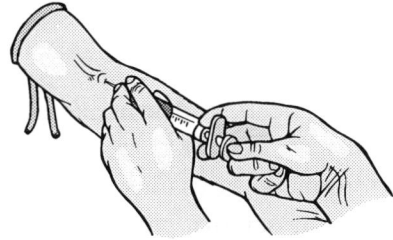

Exercise 1 (approximately 3 minutes). Following are three examples supporting the statement: Medical science has made wonderful progress in its fight against disease since 1900. Rank the examples from least impressive (oldest) to most impressive (newest) by writing the numbers 1, 2, and 3 in the spaces provided. (Vaccines were developed before transplants.)

___ Parts of the body, such as the heart and kidney, have been transplanted from one person to another.

___ Work on the ultimate medical problem, the creation of life itself, has advanced as far as test-tube babies and genetic engineering.
(*Vocabulary Tips: ultimate– most important, final; genetic engineering– creating new forms of life.*)

___ Vaccines have been developed against measles, yellow fever, and polio.
(*Vocabulary Tip: vaccine– type of medicine taken to prevent a disease.*)

Exercise 2 (approximately 7 minutes). The three sentences you just ranked have been reproduced along with seven others below. Number the sentences to form a paragraph with the following arrangement:

- Begin with a generalization about progress in our century compared to earlier times.

- Present one supporting statement followed by several examples and then another supporting statement with its examples.

- Close with a sentence that reinforces the opening generalization by comparing the 20th century favorably with later time periods.

___ For example, medical science has made wonderful progress in its fight against disease since 1900.

___ Also, parts of the body, such as the heart and kidney, have been transplanted from one person to another.

___ Even work on the ultimate medical problem, the creation of life itself, has advanced as far as test-tube babies and genetic engineering.

___ Most recently, nuclear energy has been harnessed to provide electrical power for homes and industry, and computers have been developed that solve problems faster than the human brain.

___ Astounding progress has been made outside of medicine as well.

___ Considering it took humans thousands of years to learn to make simple tools like knives and plows out of iron, the scientific and technical advances of our own century are spectacular.
(*Vocabulary Tips: century–100 years; spectacular– terrific, striking, sensational.*)

___ One can hardly imagine any future century being more innovative than ours, the 20th Century.
(*Vocabulary Tips: innovative– producing new things, original, creative; 20th Century– 100 years from 1901-2000.*)

___ Airplanes have been invented, jet engines have made air travel faster, and rockets have carried men to the moon.

___ Vaccines have been developed against measles, yellow fever, and polio.

___ The 20th Century has given us copy machines, televisions, and compact discs.

Exercise 3 (approximately 15 minutes). Write the sentences in the order you numbered them to form a long paragraph on progress in our century.

_____

_____

_____

_____

_____

_____

_____

Section 7
Buyer Beware

Do you believe the promises made in magazine advertisements? The following sentences can be organized into a paper claiming that much advertising is false.

Exercises

Exercise 1 (approximately 15 minutes). Number the sentences within each paragraph to form the best logical order.

First Paragraph

____ Millions of teenagers as well as adults believe these ads and send in their dollars for the promise of a lovelier figure or quick weight loss.

____ Magazines are filled with advertisements promising spectacular improvements in your appearance quickly and with little effort.

____ But unfortunately the only people who benefit from most of the advertised miracle products are the fast-buck salesmen who collect the cash.

Second Paragraph

____ As soon as you drink any liquid, the weight returns to exactly the body area where it was originally.

_2_ The ads say they will take two inches off your waist or hips in just hours.

____ Rubber waist bands and plastic shorts, sometimes called "spot reducers," are prime examples of such money-making gimmicks.

____ In short, the spot reducers are not just worthless; they can be hazardous.

_4_ But medical studies show that weight loss from sweating is not permanent.

____ They work by causing excessive sweating in the part of the body covered.

____ What is worse, the tight rubber (or plastic) clothing can interfere with normal circulation, leading to blood clots, and can make the body overheat to a dangerous degree.

Third Paragraph

___2___ The Food and Drug Administration warns that most ingredients sold for weight control without a prescription have not been shown to be effective and can also be dangerous.

_____ The FDA concluded that diet pills should not be used for more than three months, and that a permanent weight loss will only occur if a person changes his or her eating habits.

_____ In fact, out of 111 ingredients contained in over-the-counter weight-control drugs, the FDA found that only two were effective.

_____ One ingredient, benzocaine, dulls the nerve endings in the mouth.

_____ Another group of widely advertised quick cure products are diet pills.

_____ The other, phenylpropanolamin hydrochloride, curbs the appetite but also raises blood pressure, which is potentially dangerous.

Fourth Paragraph

_____ The safest way to protect yourself against false advertising is to remember that whenever a product seems "too good to be true," it probably is just that.

Exercise 2 (approximately 10 minutes). Write the sentences in the order you numbered them to form a paper cautioning consumers.

Section 8
Misplaced Convention Center

Do you always agree with government decisions? When you disagree, can you write a clear explanation of your reasons in order to convince others of your opinion? The following sentences can be arranged to explain several reasons why the writer disagrees with a city council decision.

Exercise

Exercise (approximately 15 minutes). Number the sentences within each paragraph to form the best logical order.

First Paragraph

____ Now it is almost completed, and I loathe it.
(Vocabulary Tip: loathe– hate.)

____ The primary reasons for my attitude are that the chosen site mars the beach's inherent beauty and ability to draw tourists; it wastes an opportunity for economic growth in the western, inland section of town; and it strains the beach's natural and man-made environments almost to the point of destruction.
(Vocabulary Tips: site– location; inherent– built-in, natural.)

____ Last year the officials of my city, Daytona Beach, Florida, voted to build a new convention center right across from the ocean.
(Vocabulary Tip: convention center– large building used for big meetings, shows, and other events.)

Second Paragraph

____ People will pay top dollar to temporarily or permanently live by the sea.

____ Wherever there is a beach, you are sure to find competition to use all of the available space.

_3_ The space taken by the convention center could have been used to build an attractive beach-side hotel or apartment complex that would have drawn additional tourists to the town and fully utilized the economic potential of beach property.

____ Had the city officials used greater foresight in planning, the area could have become a showcase for the entire East Coast with a free-spending tourist population to match.
(Vocabulary Tip: foresight– concern and good planning for the future.)

The Whimbey Writing Program - Student Workbook **127**

___ Moreover, viewing the ocean at sunrise, or under a full moon, or during a violent storm—these wonderful experiences were lost for countless people when a convention center was built instead of living rooms and bedrooms overlooking the Atlantic.

Third Paragraph

___ A westward location would have permitted the center's patrons to be closer to the array of attractions already in that area.
(*Vocabulary Tip: patron*– *customer.*)

___ Next, the chosen site wastes an opportunity for the economic development of the inland area west of the beach.

_3_ These attractions (dog track, jai alai games, auto racing, two shopping malls, and several restaurants) are tailor-made for the partying and shopping needs of conventioneers.

___ In this and other ways, a western site would have raised the value of a large parcel of land that does not have the natural premium value of beach property.
(*Vocabulary Tip: premium*– *best, special, expensive.*)

___ All of these businesses would have benefited from the increased patronage by conventioneers, and additional businesses could have been built because there is plenty of room for expansion on the inland side of town.

Fourth Paragraph

___ When an audience packs in for a rock concert, the smells created by the trash and sewerage will mask those of the fresh salt air; the noises from heavy traffic will drown out the sounds of the waves; and the view of the seashore will be less enjoyable with 15,000 extra people milling about.

___ Finally, the most devastating problem is the strain that the chosen site will put on the natural and man-made resources of this area.

___ The natural resource is the beach, with its view, its smells, its sounds, and its shoreline.

Fifth Paragraph

___ The next bridge has four lanes, but it too was built at least 40 years ago.

___ Because the site, like most Florida east coast beaches, is located on a long, narrow island separated from the mainland by a river, it can be reached only by bridge.

___ A major strain will also be placed on the man-made resources.

___ The road and bridge closest to the new center are only two lanes wide and very old.

___5___ It will be a traffic nightmare when crowds merge at these bridges to get across the river to attend an event at the convention center.
(*Vocabulary Tip: merge– join together.*)

_____ However, the collapse of one of the bridges should be a concern for everyone who plans to use them either to attend a major event or to travel to and from the beach.

_____ I hope it is only minor fender benders and impatience that these people will have to face.

Sixth Paragraph

_____ But the beach is unique with pleasures that cannot be duplicated or enhanced except by keeping the surrounding areas clean and well maintained.
(*Vocabulary Tip: enhanced– made larger or better.*)

_____ All in all, I wish the beach area had been left alone to be enjoyed as "the beach."

_____ It is a shame that those in power did not realize this before it was too late.

_____ The monstrosity of concrete and glass could have gone elsewhere and been patronized just as well.
(*Vocabulary Tip: monstrosity– large, abnormal thing, freak.*)

Section 9
Analysis of Generalization-Specifics Papers

This chapter illustrated paragraphs and papers organized in the generalization-specifics pattern. As shown in sections 4 through 8, a persuasive 250-600 word paper of this type usually includes at least three pieces of specific supporting evidence. And each of these is backed up with even more specific examples. Specific details expand on a generalization, capturing the reader's imagination and clarifying the writer's meaning.

Starting a Generalization-Specifics Paper. Section 3 (Credit Cards) involved a short paper (around 250 words) that did not have a separate introductory paragraph. The generalization was stated, and then the first supporting detail was immediately described in the opening paragraph. Section 7 (Buyer Beware) had a longer paper of around 350 words. The entire opening paragraph was devoted to introducing the generalization and to providing a little background information. Section 8 (Convention Center) had an opening paragraph that not only introduced the generalization but also previewed the three specific points used to support it. This is an effective way to begin a generalization-specifics paper; it is discussed extensively in the next chapter.

Defending an Opinion. Sometimes a generalization is an opinion that others might disagree with. A good way to begin such a paper is to mention the opposing arguments in the introduction, but then to show how your position deals with them. An example of this was seen in Section 4; the paper began, "It is true that new trucks are expensive and the family budget is tight." In this way the writer acknowledged the financial problems of buying a new truck and then addressed them in the paper.

The Hermit Crab paper took a somewhat different approach. Because the thesis was that a hermit crab is the best of all possible pets, the paper contrasted hermits with other common pets to show their virtues regarding cost and convenience. In this way the writer tried to anticipate some of the arguments from lovers of other pets.

Ending a Generalization-Specifics Paper. An important caution should be noted on how not to end a generalization-specifics paper. Do not introduce a new idea in the conclusion. Inexperienced writers sometimes cannot think of how to end a paper, so they start off on a new point. In the Credit Card paper, an inexperienced writer might think it would make the ending more interesting to say that traveler's cheques also are useful. But such an ending is unconvincing because there is no opportunity to support the new idea with examples and specific details.

It is better to end a paper of this type by simply summarizing your generalization and perhaps tying it together with some of your specific support. For a short paper, this usually can be done with one sentence. The Credit Card paper ended, "In short, a credit card gives you all the purchasing power of continually carrying several hundred dollars, but none of the risk." When you can avoid a phrase like "in short" or "in summary," it is better to do so because these phrases are used very often in papers. The False Advertising paper illustrates a closing sentence that does not use a phrase like "in summary," but still does summarize the main idea of the paper: "The safest way to protect yourself against false advertising is to remember that whenever a product seems 'too good to be true,' it probably is just that."

The Hermit Crab and Convention Center papers were longer—over 450 words—so they used separate paragraphs for conclusions. The Convention Center paper summarized the main ideas in a final paragraph this way:

> All in all, I wish the beach area had been left alone to be enjoyed as "the beach." The monstrosity of concrete and glass could have gone elsewhere and been patronized just as well. But the beach is unique with pleasures that cannot be duplicated or enhanced except by keeping the surrounding areas clean and well maintained. It is a shame that those in power did not realize this before it was too late.

Notice that this paragraph does not introduce any new ideas. Instead, it strongly restates the author's opinion and summarizes some of the supporting arguments.

In the present chapter you arranged sentences into generalization-specifics papers. Because this is such an important writing pattern, the next two chapters are devoted to helping you write your own original papers of this type.

Chapter 7
Beginning with a Thesis Statement

This chapter teaches a technique for writing a paper that convincingly defends an opinion. The ability to write such a paper is useful when you are trying to sway people to take some action. It also is useful in writing papers to pass writing competency tests and meet course requirements.

The technique consists of starting with a thesis statement that presents an opinion and also lists the evidence supporting it. The remainder of the paper explains the supporting evidence with specific details. This unit takes you through the steps of applying the technique in writing your own papers.

Section 1
Two Parts of the Thesis Statement

The first step is to write the thesis statement. Your thesis statement is a summary of your entire paper. It states an opinion or point of view and also previews the evidence you will use to support that opinion. Here is an example of a thesis statement:

- Daytona Beach is a great place to take a vacation because of its warm climate, good beaches, reasonably priced motels, and major auto/cycle race track.

Notice that this thesis statement has two parts: a statement of opinion and a list of the supporting evidence. Here are the two parts:

1. Statement of opinion: Daytona Beach is a great place to take a vacation.

2. Supporting evidence: warm climate, good beaches, reasonably priced motels, major race track.

Exercises

Now try these exercises.

Exercise 1 (approximately 3 minutes). Write the two parts of the following thesis statement in the spaces.

- Thesis Statement: Swimming is one of the best forms of exercise since it tones the muscles, decreases the risk of heart attack, and does not strain the back or joints.

- Statement of opinion: _____

- Supporting evidence: _____
  _____

Exercise 2 (approximately 3 minutes). Write the two parts of the following thesis statement in the spaces provided.

- Thesis Statement: New York City is a wonderful place to live because it has good public transportation; a wide range of job opportunities; many schools and colleges; thousands of movies, theaters, and restaurants; and many fine museums.

132   Beginning with a Thesis Statement

- Statement of opinion: _____

- Supporting evidence: _____

  _____

Section 2
Writing Your Thesis Statement

If you are like most people, you have many opinions. You believe some things are good or worthwhile, whereas others are bad or useless. Perhaps you think a certain baseball star is the best player who ever lived, that a certain car would suit your needs perfectly, or that some city would be nice to visit. Maybe you dislike some teacher, school subject, or occupation. Perhaps you feel cigarettes should be taxed at $20 a pack. Use one of your opinions for the next exercise.

Exercise

| Opinion |
| Evidence #1 |
| Evidence #2 |

Exercise (approximately 10 minutes). Pick one of your opinions that you can support with at least two pieces of evidence. Write the opinion and supporting evidence in the form of a thesis statement.

Thesis Statement: _____

_____

_____

_____

_____

_____

_____

_____

The Whimbey Writing Program - Student Workbook

Section 3
Presenting Specific Details for the Supporting Evidence

The second step is to write one or more paragraphs giving details to explain each piece of supporting evidence in your thesis statement. Here is how this could be done for the thesis statement about Daytona Beach:

> Daytona Beach is a great place to take a vacation because of its warm climate, good beaches, reasonably priced motels, absence of traffic problems, and major car/cycle race track.
>
> The climate in Daytona is warm; snow is virtually unknown. While the northern states are slick with ice in January and February, the daytime temperature in Daytona averages around 70 degrees, permitting people to sunbathe and go boating or fishing. By March, the temperature climbs to 80 degrees, and the ocean is warm enough for swimming. Even in the evening the temperature is mild enough that all you need is a sweater to go out and have dinner or fun at the beach parties.
>
> Daytona has a 15-mile strip of beach that is free to the public. Furthermore, you can drive onto the beach, park your car, and put your blanket or beach chair beside it. Thus you avoid paying high parking fees, or searching for an hour to find a parking space and then walking many blocks to reach the ocean.

To complete this paper you would write one paragraph on the reasonable prices of motels and another paragraph on the excitement of the car and cycle races. Finally, you would write a conclusion paragraph that summarizes your main points.

If your thesis statement only listed two pieces of supporting evidence, then you should present more details for each one in order to defend your opinion. For example, in the preceding paper you might spend several paragraphs describing the pleasures of the warm climate and the fun on the beach. Now it is your turn; try the exercise.

Exercise

```
Evidence #1
  Details
Evidence #2
  Details
Conclusion
```

Exercise (approximately 20 minutes). For each piece of evidence in your thesis statement from section 2, write at least one paragraph explaining it with examples and details. Finally, write a conclusion paragraph that summarizes your main points. (If you have difficulty writing a conclusion paragraph, review page 130).

Section 4
Taking Writing Competency Tests

The technique you just learned can be especially useful for passing writing competency tests. On such tests you generally are given a list of broad topics. You are asked to pick one topic and write a paper on it. Try these steps:

- Pick a topic on which you have a viewpoint or opinion that you can support with several examples or pieces of evidence.

- Write a thesis statement of the type presented in this chapter.

- Make sure to present enough details and examples to fully explain and illustrate each of your supporting points.

- Write a conclusion paragraph that summarizes your main points.

If you follow these steps and use standard, grammatically correct English, your papers will be seen as well organized and well written. The next chapter provides additional guidance in writing a paper of this type.

Remember, however, that you are not required to use the opinion-support pattern on many competency tests. For some tests your paper might describe a person or a place, as illustrated by papers in Chapter 1. Or your paper might describe a series of exciting or humorous actions, like the Biting Rage and The Practical "Un" Joker papers of Chapter 3. In some cases you might combine several of the patterns identified in this book. If you are asked to write a paper on any modern appliance (TV, cellular phone, microwave), you could begin with a physical description (Chapter 1), then explain its functions and provide instructions for its use (Chapter 3), and finish with several examples showing its vital role in our lives (Chapter 6). Use the combination of patterns that allows you to best express your ideas.

Chapter 8

Writing a Paper for a Competency Test: Brainstorming for Ideas

The last chapter presented a procedure for writing a paper expressing and supporting an opinion on some topic. The procedure can be used in writing to newspaper editors, congressmen, employers, or anyone else whom you are trying to convince of some viewpoint. The procedure also can be used for writing papers on exams, such as those required for admission to or graduation from many educational institutions, as well as employee selection tests given by many companies. This chapter expands on that procedure by showing you a technique you can use to get a paper started on a writing test. The technique helps you think of material that you can develop into a well-organized paper.

Section 1
What Decisions Do People Make?

Tests of writing skill often give you two or three very broad topics and ask you to write a paper of around 500 words (in about an hour) on one of the topics. Of course you may write a well-organized paper using any of the patterns covered in other chapters: cause-effect, comparison-contrast, classification, and so forth. But one of the easiest ways to write an effective paper in a limited time and without other sources of information is to use the opinion-support (also called generalization-specifics) pattern discussed in the last two chapters.

One way to help identify opinions or general statements you can express on a topic is to ask yourself, "What decisions do people make regarding the topic?" For example, suppose one of the broad topics is getting a job. What decisions do people face and what questions do they have on the topic of getting a job?

> Should I get a job?
> How will I get to work?
> Do I have the skills to get hired?
> How will I keep up with my school work?
> Will I still have some free time?
> What would be the best job for me?
> What will I do with the money?

Now place yourself in the position of answering the questions and making the decisions. How would you decide and why? What factors do you consider important in the job you choose?

Your answers to these questions—your opinions—are candidates for a 500-word paper. But before going on to the next step, try these exercises.

Exercises

Exercise 1 (approximately 5 minutes). Write at least five decisions and questions that you think a person might face on the topic, "Going to College."

Broad Topic: Going to College

Question 1:_____

138 *Writing a Paper for a Competency Test*

Question 2: _____

Question 3: _____

Question 4: _____

Question 5: _____

Exercise 2 (approximately 5 minutes). Write at least five decisions and questions that you think a person might face on the topic, "Playing a High School Sport."

Broad Topic: Playing a High School Sport

Question 1: _____

Question 2: _____

Question 3: _____

Question 4: _____

Question 5: _____

Exercise 3 (approximately 5 minutes). Write at least five decisions and questions that you think a person might face on the topic, "Careers that Interest Me."

Broad Topic: Careers That Interest Me

Question 1: _____

Question 2: _____

Question 3: _____

Question 4: _____

Question 5: _____

Exercise 4 (approximately 5 minutes). Write at least five decisions and questions that you think a person might face on the topic, "Good and Bad Things about Living in My Town."

Broad Topic: Good and Bad Things about Living in My Town

Question 1:_____

Question 2: _____

Question 3: _____

Question 4: _____

Question 5: _____

Section 2
Brainstorming for Information and Opinions

Do you have any opinions or information about the questions you wrote in the last section? If you immediately think of an opinion or answer to one of the questions (which you can support with several examples), you may be ready to begin writing a paper.

But if you do not immediately think of anything useful, try brainstorming about the questions you wrote. "Brainstorming" means letting as many ideas as possible come into your mind and writing them down quickly without judging or trying to organize them. Here are some questions that were written earlier on getting a job. Next to them is a list of ideas that came to mind while brainstorming about these questions. Notice that the ideas from brainstorming are not written in sentences. They are just written as quickly as they come to mind.

Decisions & Questions	Ideas from Brainstorming
Where can I get a job?	fast-food places, movie theater, ice cream store, work with dad
Do I have the skills to get hired?	hardworking, punctual, smart, presentable
How will I get to work?	take bus, ride bike, get rides from parents and friends
How will I keep up with my schoolwork?	Work only 20 hours per week, work on weekends, no late hours
What will I do with the money I earn?	car, clothes, gifts for girlfriend, movies
What would be the best job for me to get?	easy, fun, interesting, good pay, helping others

Will I still have some free time?	less time for friends, watch less television, make better use of free time

The brainstorming list may now contain enough ideas for a paper. The next step is to try to use some of them in writing a thesis statement. But first do the following brainstorming exercises.

Exercises

Exercise 1 (approximately 10 minutes). In the last section you wrote your own questions about decisions related to the topic "Going to College." Some sample questions are presented below. Read them, then brainstorm for ideas related to these questions and the questions you wrote earlier.

General Topic: Going to College

<u>Sample Questions</u>   <u>Brainstorming Ideas</u>

Why should I go to college?   _____

How will I pay for college?   _____

_____   _____

_____   _____

_____   _____

Which college should I attend?   _____

What factors are important in picking a
college?   _____

What should I major in at college?   _____

What factors should I consider in selecting
a major?   _____

Exercise 2 (approximately 10 minutes). Here are some sample questions about decisions related to the topic "Playing a School Sport." Brainstorm for ideas related to these questions and the questions you wrote earlier.

General Topic: Playing a School Sport

Sample Questions   Brainstorming Ideas

Should I play a school sport?   _____

What are the benefits of playing a school
sport?   _____

What are the disadvantages of playing a
school sport?   _____

What sport should I play?   _____

Are women given an equal chance?   _____

_____   _____

_____   _____

Exercise 3 (approximately 10 minutes). Here are some sample questions about decisions related to the topic "Careers That Interest Me." Brainstorm for ideas and answers to these questions and the questions you wrote earlier.

General Topic: Careers That Interest Me

Sample Questions   Brainstorming Ideas

Which career should I choose?   _____

Which careers will offer me the income
I desire?   _____

Which career would I enjoy?   _____

For which careers do I have the education
or preparation to start work immediately?   _____

Which careers require more than
just a high school diploma?

_____   _____

_____   _____

Exercise 4 (approximately 10 minutes). Here are some sample questions about decisions related to the topic "Good and Bad Things About Living in My Town." Brainstorm for ideas related to these questions and the questions you wrote earlier.

General Topic: Good and Bad Things About Living in My Town

<u>Sample Questions</u>   <u>Brainstorming Ideas</u>

Is my town a desirable place to live?   _____

What are the employment opportunities
in my town?   _____

What are the entertainment and
social attractions of my town?   _____

How expensive is housing in my town?   _____

What is the climate in my town?   _____

_____   _____

_____   _____

Section 3
Writing a Thesis Statement

After brainstorming for ideas on a topic, you are ready to try to write a thesis statement. One of the easiest thesis statements to write and support with examples is the statement that certain factors should be considered in making a particular decision. Here is an example for the topic, "Getting a Job."

> There are several important considerations in getting a job, including the type and hours of work, the salary, and juggling work and other interests and responsibilities.

The thesis statement above merely presented factors that should be considered in making a decision about getting a job; it did not express an opinion about an important decision. A second type of thesis statement does express an opinion about a decision, which it supports with evidence. Here are two examples based on the brainstorming list:

> Getting a job is an excellent way to earn money for college and get work experience at the same time.

> Unless you would like to work at a fast-food restaurant as a career, it is a good idea to spend a little more time job-hunting to find a job in a career field that interests you.

Now try the following exercises in which you will write thesis statements based on your own brainstorming.

Exercises

Exercise 1 (approximately 10 minutes). Using your brainstorming list from the last section, write the following two types of thesis statements about going to college.

Thesis Statement 1: Write a thesis statement on factors that should be considered in some decision about going to college.

_____

_____

Thesis Statement 2: Write a thesis statement expressing an opinion supported by two or more pieces of evidence regarding a decision about going to college.

_____

_____

Exercise 2 (approximately 10 minutes). Same as exercise 1 for the topic, "Playing a School Sport."

Thesis Statement 1: _____

_____

_____

Thesis Statement 2: _____

_____

_____

Exercise 3 (approximately 10 minutes). Same as exercise 1 for the topic, "Careers that Interest Me."

Thesis Statement 1: _____

_____

_____

Thesis Statement 2: _____

_____

_____

Exercise 4 (approximately 10 minutes). Same as exercise 1 for the topic, "Good and Bad Things About Living in My Town."

Thesis Statement 1: _____

_____

_____

Thesis Statement 2: _____

_____

_____

Section 4
Writing a Thesis Paragraph to Express a Mixed Opinion

If you want to express a mixed opinion—both the good and bad sides of an issue—you may need more than one sentence to do the job of the thesis statement, namely, to state the opinion and also preview the supporting evidence. Here is an example of a mixed opinion and its supporting evidence expressed in a four-sentence paragraph.

> Living in Manhattan has both good and bad points. On the positive side, there are endless employment, cultural, and entertainment opportunities. But you never get away from the noise of people and machines, and there is no chance to enjoy nature. In fact, because of the traffic congestion and parking problems, you can't even enjoy the pleasure of driving your own car to work, to stores, or to go out with friends.

Write similar paragraphs for the next exercises.

Exercises

Exercise 1 (approximately 5 minutes). Number the following sentences so they first express a mixed attitude on a topic and then preview the supporting details.

____ Having a job will mean less time for school extracurricular activities.

____ Finally, going to work will offer the chance to get some professional experience.

____ There are disadvantages and advantages to getting a job while still in school.

____ But having a job will mean a lot of extra spending money.

____ And there will be less time to spend with friends.

Exercise 2 (approximately 10 minutes). Following is a list of attractions and drawbacks of living in Daytona Beach. Write a short paragraph expressing a mixed opinion about living in Daytona and previewing the supporting evidence.

Attractions: mild year-round climate; good beaches, golf courses, tennis courts and other outdoor recreational facilities; major auto/cycle track; relaxed tourist-town atmosphere.

146 Writing a Paper for a Competency Test

Drawbacks: limited industry and employment opportunities; weak on cultural facilities like museums, theaters, libraries, and fine restaurants; no snow or ice sports; snow really missed at Christmas; tourists cause severe traffic jams during racing season and spring break.

___

Exercise 3 (approximately 10 minutes). Write a short paragraph expressing a mixed opinion and previewing the supporting evidence on one of these topics: Going to College; Playing a School Sport; Careers That Interest Me; Living in My Town.

___

Section 5
Writing and Checking the Final Paper

Once you have written the thesis statement or paragraph, writing the complete paper simply involves adding several paragraphs with your supporting details, along with an introductory paragraph to arouse interest, and a conclusion paragraph to summarize your main ideas. For each of your supporting paragraphs, include specific examples (with names, prices, or other information) to make your ideas clear and convincing.

Before you actually begin to write the paper, it is a good idea to spend about ten minutes making a rough paragraph-by-paragraph outline. For each paragraph, write down the examples and details that you will use to support your ideas. If any good sentences expressing your ideas come to mind, write them down for later use. Preparing an outline (even a rough one) will make the job of writing your paper much easier.

One final note: As you write the paper, plan to save about five minutes to re-read and check. You will usually find some spelling and grammatical errors. You may even see a better way to express an idea. Your paper will make a stronger impression if you take the time to polish off its rough edges.

Section 6
Planning Your Exam Time

Here is the way you might allot your time for a 50-minute writing exam. Make appropriate adjustments if you are allowed only 30 minutes or a whole hour.

1. (5 minutes.) Decide whether you can make a statement or express an opinion about one of the topics which you can illustrate or support with three paragraphs of information and details. If you can, go straight to step 3. If no such ideas come to mind immediately, pick one topic and start writing down decisions and questions about it. If other ideas or information about the topic come to mind, write them down also.
2. (3 minutes.) Brainstorm for answers and information to the questions from stage 1. Write down all ideas that come to mind. They might be useful later.
3. (3 minutes.) Write a thesis statement that expresses your position and previews the supporting material.
4. (9 minutes.) Make a rough, paragraph-by-paragraph outline. Think of concrete examples that can be used for each paragraph. Also, think about how you would introduce or express

ideas. If any good sentences come to mind, write them down. Include all of this in your outline.

5. (25 minutes.) Write the paper using your outline. Include a short introductory paragraph to arouse interest and a conclusion paragraph to summarize your position.
6. (5 minutes.) Read the entire paper carefully for spelling and grammatical errors; also look for awkward phrasing that could be improved.

Now try the exercise below.

Exercise

Exercise (approximately 50 minutes). Treat this exercise like a writing competency exam with a 50-minute time limit. Write a paper of about 500 words on one of the following topics:

    Going to College
    Nuclear Energy
    Playing a School Sport
    School and Drugs
    Careers That Interest Me
    Living in My Town

_____

_____

_____

_____

_____

_____

_____

_____

_____

_____

Section 7
Other Competency-Test Papers

If the opinion-support pattern does not fit the topics on a competency test, use another pattern or a mixture of patterns. For example, suppose one of the topics is: "Describe and discuss an invention of the past 100 years." If you decide to write about the airplane, you might begin with a physical description of an airplane (Chapter 1), then include some material on its history or operation (Chapter 3), and finally present examples to show its importance (Chapter 6). Or, if a topic lends itself to a description of a place or a person, you might present a physical description interwoven with human actions and reactions, as illustrated in the School Cafeteria and Steel Drums papers of Chapter 1. Use any combination of patterns that fits the topic.

Chapter 9
Comparing and Contrasting

When you compare two things, you describe their similarities. When you contrast them, you describe their differences. A comparison/contrast paper generally compares and contrasts two things on a number of points, showing how they are alike in some ways and different in others. One way to begin a comparison/contrast paper is with a chart like this for James Bond (Agent 007) and Superman.

	James Bond	vs.	Superman
similarities	1. fictitious superhero 2. attractive male 3. fights crime 4. always wins	⟷ ⟷ ⟷ ⟷	fictitious superhero attractive male fights crime always wins
differences	5. fights crime for pay and country 6. no disguises 7. enjoys the company of women 8. uses technology extensively: modern weapons, sport cars, helicopters, tricky devices	≠ ≠ ≠ ≠	fights crime for justice and mankind two identities secretly and shyly loves Lois Lane depends on own power: superhuman strength, ability to fly, x-ray vision, bullet-proof body

When you make a chart like this, the ideas generally will not come into your mind all neatly arranged with the similarities first and then the differences. Instead, the ideas may come somewhat haphazardly. But write down all the ideas as you think of them so you won't forget them. Later you can arrange them according to similarities and differences as well as their importance and human interest value.

Once you have a chart, you are almost ready to begin a comparison/contrast paper. But you still have a decision. Should you write all about one superhero first and then all about the other one, as pictured below?

- Block-by-Block Organization

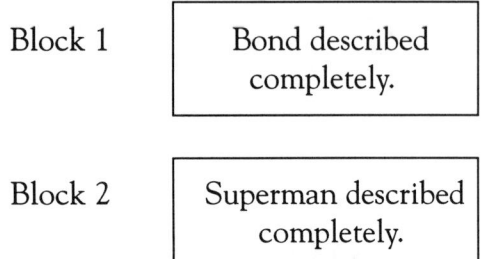

Block 1 — Bond described completely.

Block 2 — Superman described completely.

Or should you describe Bond and Superman on point 1, then Bond and Superman on point 2, and so on, covering the points of similarity in the early paragraphs and the differences in the later ones?

- Point-by-Point Organization

    Bond similar to Superman on point 1.
    Bond similar to Superman on point 2.
    Bond similar to Superman on point 3.
    Bond similar to Superman on point 4.

    Bond different from Superman on point 5.
    Bond different from Superman on point 6.
    Bond different from Superman on point 7.
    Bond different from Superman on point 8.

The first type of paper is called a Block-by-Block pattern, whereas the second is a Point-by-Point.

In deciding on a topic for a comparison/contrast paper, pick things that are somewhat similar. It is easier to compare a Chevy with a Cadillac than an airplane with an apple. In a real-life business situation, your boss is more likely to ask for a comparison/contrast report on two models of typewriters rather than a comparison/contrast between a typewriter and a copy machine.

As you work through the exercises of this chapter, remember you are sharpening a skill that many people use to earn good incomes by writing comparison/contrast reports of products for magazines, handbooks, and manuals published by most large companies.

Section 1
Comparison or Contrast?

When you compare two things, you describe their similarities. When you contrast them, you focus on their differences. This is illustrated in the following sentences.

Exercise

Exercise (approximately 10 minutes). Five of the following sentences make comparisons, pointing out similarities between two things. The other four are contrasts, highlighting differences. Decide whether each sentence forms a comparison or contrast, and then write it in the appropriate space.

1. A microphone and a human ear are both sensitive to the small movements of the air produced when any sound is made.

2. The ball used in ping pong is smaller and lighter than the one used in tennis.

3. The *New York Times* and the *New York Post* are two high-circulation newspapers.

4. A sedan has four doors, whereas a coupe has only two doors.

5. Brick cheese is solid white, but blue cheese has bluish-green veins.

6. The world supply of oil and the supply of coal will eventually be exhausted. (*Vocabulary Tip: exhausted– used up.*)

7. Spanish is the official language in many South American countries as well as in Spain.

8. A door and a bottle cap share the purpose of keeping things in or out.

9. Pedro had a better opportunity to get an education than his older brother did.

Comparison Sentences (highlighting similarities)

1. _____
2. _____

3. _____

4. _____

5. _____

Contrast Sentences (highlighting differences)

1. _____

2. _____

3. _____

4. _____

Section 2
Comparison and Contrast Paragraph

The following sentences can be arranged into a paragraph that compares and contrasts two popular fruits.

Exercises

Exercise 1 (approximately 5 minutes). Number the sentences in the best logical order, with the first three comparing plums to peaches and the remaining three contrasting them. One sentence has already been numbered 2.

____ Moreover, plums are generally all one color—either red or purple—whereas peaches are multicolored: red, yellow, and a light shade of orange named "peach."

____ Both fruits are juicy and sweet when properly ripened.

____ Finally, each has a distinctive flavor, although this cannot be fully described but must be tasted.

__2__ They are larger than berries so people generally eat just one or two at a time, but they are smaller than melons so they are not divided and shared.

154 *Comparing and Contrasting*

___ Plums and peaches are both round, medium-sized fruits.

___ But plums have a smooth skin, whereas peaches are fuzzy.

Exercise 2 (approximately 10 minutes). Write the sentences in the order you numbered them.

_____

_____

_____

_____

_____

_____

_____

_____

Exercise 3 (approximately 15 minutes). Write a comparison/contrast paragraph on any two fruits except plums and peaches.

_____

_____

_____

_____

_____

_____

_____

_____

Section 3
Point-by-Point Contrast Paper

A paper does not have to both compare and contrast two things. It can just compare them, or it can just contrast them. The following exercises illustrate a paper that just contrasts dogs with cats. The paper is organized to contrast dogs with cats on one point or characteristic, then on a second point, and finally on a third point. Therefore, it is called a Point-by-Point contrast.

Exercises

Exercise 1 (approximately 10 minutes). The chart below shows three characteristics on which dogs can be contrasted with cats.

	Dogs	Cats
• Personal Needs	Need to be walked.	Use litter box.
• Noise	Bark, which makes them a good burglar alarm but sometimes too noisy.	Quiet.
• Companionship	Close companion to humans.	More independent of humans.

The sentences on the next page are about the three characteristics in the table. Categorize each sentence; write I, S, PN, N, or C on the line in front in this way:

- I- the sentence that could be used as an Introduction for a short paper contrasting dogs with cats.

- S- the sentence that could be used as a <u>summary</u> for the paper.

- PN- the three sentences dealing with the <u>personal needs</u> of dogs and cats.

- N- the three sentences concerning <u>noise</u>.

- C- the five sentences concerning <u>companionship</u> (not the summary sentence).

156   Comparing and Contrasting

___ All in all, dogs take a little more trouble but repay your efforts with greater companionship.

___ A cat can be trained to use a litter box in the house.

___ Second, a dog can serve as a burglar alarm, barking when anyone approaches your door.

___ If you are a city-dweller who has decided to get a pet, and you have narrowed it down to either a dog or a cat, here are some factors to consider in making the final choice.
(*Vocabulary Tip: city-dweller– person who lives in a city.*)

___ This is not an unmixed blessing, however, because the litter box can be an unpleasant sight, can produce odors in the home, and needs to be cleaned.
(*Vocabulary Tip: unmixed blessing– having only good effects.*)

___ A cat is much quieter.

___ First, a dog is a greater inconvenience because it must be walked twice a day, even when it is raining or cold outside.

___ Finally, a dog tends to be a closer companion, following you around and always glad to be petted.

___ And out of doors they are more likely to run off rather than follow you around.

___ But some dogs carry this to an extreme, annoying you and your neighbors by barking at the slightest noise anywhere nearby, or for causes totally unimaginable to humans.

___ But often they are happier to hide under the sofa rather than sit at your feet.

___ Although there are exceptions, cats are usually less friendly.

___ Occasionally they like to be petted or scratched.

Exercise 2 (approximately 15 minutes). Write the sentences as a three-paragraph paper with the following form.

- For the first paragraph, begin with the sentence you labeled I. Then write the sentences you labeled PN, describing the dog first and putting the sentences in the best logical order.

- For the second paragraph, write the sentences you labeled N. Describe the dog first and put the sentences in the best logical order.

- For the third paragraph, write the sentences you labeled C. Describe the dog first and put the sentences in the best logical order. End the paragraph with the sentence labeled S.

Section 4
Block-by-Block Contrast Paper

The paper you wrote in the last exercise contrasted dogs with cats on one point, then it contrasted them on a second point, and finally on a third point, producing a point-by-point organization.

Another way to contrast dogs with cats is to first write about dogs on all three characteristics and then write about cats, emphasizing how they differ from dogs on the three characteristics. This is called a Block-by-Block pattern. The two patterns are shown below.

- Point-by-Point Contrast

    1. Contrast dogs with cats on one characteristic or point.

    2. Contrast dogs with cats on a second point.

    3. Contrast dogs with cats on a third point.

- Block-by-Block Contrast

    1. Describe dogs on all three characteristics.

    2. Describe cats on all three characteristics, emphasizing contrasts with dogs.

Exercises

Exercise 1 (approximately 5 minutes). The sentences on the next page can be used to write a paper contrasting dogs with cats on the same three characteristics as the last exercise, but using the Block-by-Block pattern. Categorize each sentence; write I, S, D, CP, or CNC on the line in front in this way:

- I- the sentence that could be used as an <u>introduction</u> for such a paper.

- S- the sentence that could be used to <u>summarize</u> and end the paper.

- D- the three sentences that are primarily concerned with <u>dogs</u>. Be careful: One of the 12 sentences begins by describing dogs but ends with its main purpose—describing cats.

- CP- the two sentences about the <u>cat's personal</u> needs.

- CNC- the five remaining sentences. These CNC sentences are about a <u>cat's noise</u> and <u>companionship</u>.

____ A cat, by contrast, does not need to be walked daily but can be trained to use a litter box in the house.

____ But on the positive side, a dog can serve as a good burglar alarm, barking when anyone approaches your door.

____ This is not an unmixed blessing, however, because the litter box can be an unpleasant sight, can produce odors in the house, and needs to be cleaned.

____ A dog also tends to be a closer companion, following you around, always glad to be petted, and often barking or nudging you to play.

____ As opposed to the silly antics and noisiness of many dogs, a cat is a nice quiet roommate. (*Vocabulary Tip: antics– clownish behavior.*)

____ Man's best friend, the dog, is a greater inconvenience because it must be walked twice a day, even when it is raining or cold outside.

____ And it doesn't constantly pester you for attention.

____ It doesn't bark every time anything passes anywhere near your home, driving you and your neighbors to distraction.

____ All in all, a cat provides pleasant although cooler companionship than a dog, and it intrudes less on your time and other activities.

____ If you are a city dweller who has decided to buy a pet, and you have narrowed it down to either a dog or a cat, here are some major considerations in making the final choice.

____ Occasionally it greets you or comes over for pets and scratches.

____ But generally it respects your right to privacy and is content to live with you in peaceful coexistence.

Exercise 2 (approximately 15 minutes). Write the sentences in the form of a three-paragraph paper. For the first paragraph, begin with the sentence you labeled I, then write the sentences labeled D in the best logical order. For the second paragraph, write the sentences labeled CP in the best logical order. For the third paragraph, write the CNC sentences in the best logical order. Finish with the sentence labeled S.

_____

_____

Section 5
Chocolate Freaks Take Note

If you like chocolate, you are not alone. However, do you know about another product, carob, that is used in place of chocolate but is much healthier? This is the subject of the following comparison/contrast paper.

Exercises

Exercise 1 (approximately 10 minutes). The sentences in the first paragraph describe similarities between chocolate and carob. The second and third paragraphs describe differences. Number the sentences within each paragraph to form the best logical order.

First Paragraph

____ But another substance called carob is similar enough in flavor that it can be substituted for chocolate in most recipes.

____ To make chocolate, the seeds are dried, roasted, and ground into a brown powder.

____ For example, you can buy chocolate chip cookies or carob chip cookies, chocolate brownies or carob brownies, chocolate or carob ice cream, chocolate or carob shakes and hot drinks, and chocolate or carob candy bars.

____ Most people like chocolate.

____ For carob, the pods go through the same process, producing a brown flour.

____ Both chocolate and carob come from trees with large pods containing seeds.
(*Vocabulary Tip: pod– plant part containing seeds.*)

Second Paragraph

____ Furthermore, chocolate is naturally bitter whereas carob is sweet.

____ First, chocolate contains more natural fat than carob—about 52% fat in chocolate compared to only 2% in carob—making it higher in calories.

____ Therefore, a greater quantity of sugar is required to make chocolate tasty, and this contributes additional calories.

162   *Comparing and Contrasting*

___ Although carob and chocolate are similar in appearance and taste, carob is healthier for a number of reasons.

___ Besides fewer calories, another advantage of carob is that it is rich in protein, vitamins A and B, and the minerals phosphorus and calcium.

___ Instead it contains caffeine, a stimulant which, in large quantities, can make a person nervous or jittery.

___ Chocolate also gives many people upset stomachs and allergic reactions.

___ Chocolate, by contrast, has no such nutrients.
(*Vocabulary Tip: nutrients– ingredients that provide nourishment.*)

Third Paragraph

___ In fact, about 2 billion pounds of chocolate are consumed in the United States annually, much more than the amount of carob eaten.

___ Only time will show whether carob can overtake chocolate in popularity.

___ Despite the health advantages of carob, at present most people choose chocolate products because they prefer its flavor.

Exercise 2 (approximately 15 minutes). Write the sentences in the order you numbered them to form a short Point-by-Point comparison/contrast paper on chocolate and carob.

_____

_____

_____

_____

_____

_____

_____

_____

_____

Exercise 3 (approximately 10 minutes). The sentences in the first paragraph below describe chocolate. The second paragraph describes carob, and the third describes the relative popularity of the two flavors. Number the sentences within each paragraph to form the best logical order.

First Paragraph

___ The seeds are dried, roasted, ground into a powder, and then made into consumer products.

___ It is used in making brownies, chocolate ice cream, chocolate shakes and hot drinks, chocolate chip cookies, and, of course, chocolate candy bars.

___ Most people like chocolate.

_3_ Chocolate comes from a tree with large seedpods.

___ Unfortunately for dieters, chocolate contains about 52% fat, which makes it high in calories.

_7_ Other than fat, chocolate has no nutrients.

___ Furthermore, because it is naturally bitter, large quantities of sugar must be used to make it tasty, and this contributes additional calories.

164 Comparing and Contrasting

___ Another drawback of chocolate is that it causes upset stomachs and allergic reactions in many people.

___ Instead, it contains caffeine, a stimulant which, in large quantities, can make a person nervous or jittery.

Second Paragraph

___ But for carob, the pods rather than the seeds are dried, roasted, and ground into a brown flour.

___ For example, you can buy carob brownies, ice cream, shakes, hot drinks, carob chip cookies, and carob candy bars.

___ Because of chocolate's disadvantages, many nutrition experts recommend another substance called carob, which is similar enough in flavor that it can be substituted for chocolate in most recipes.

___ Carob contains only 2% fat, making it lower in calories than chocolate.

___ Like chocolate, carob comes from a seedpod-bearing tree.

___ Another advantage of carob is that it is a nutritious food, rich in protein, vitamins A and B, and the minerals phosphorus and calcium.

___ Finally, carob does not contain caffeine, nor does it cause upset stomachs or allergic reactions.

___ Furthermore, it is naturally sweet, so little if any sugar needs to be added to make it tasty, saving even more calories.

Third Paragraph

___ But it isn't.

___ It seems chocolate has an evil grip on people's taste buds, and carob doesn't have enough "flavor power" to break the spell.

___ In fact, about 2 billion pounds of chocolate are eaten in the United States each year, many times the amount of carob consumed.

___ With all of carob's health advantages, you might expect it to be consumed in larger quantities than chocolate.

Exercise 4 (approximately 15 minutes). Write the sentences in the order you numbered them to form a short Block-by-Block comparison/contrast paper on chocolate and carob.

Exercise 5 (approximately 35 minutes). Prepare an outline based on the example below, exercises 2 and 4, and your own experiences with chocolate and carob. Then put away other materials and write a comparison/contrast paper on chocolate and carob. Remember that you generally must write a paper twice before it is well-organized, well-written, and fit for others to read.

<u>Outline of Chocolate vs. Carob</u>

- <u>Similarities</u>. Both used in brownies, ice cream, cookies, etc. Both from trees with seedpods. For chocolate, seeds are dried, roasted, and ground into powder. For carob, pods are dried, roasted, and powdered.

- <u>Differences</u>. Carob healthier: Lower in fat (2% vs. 52%); not bitter (so less sugar added); contains protein, vitamins A and B, minerals phosphorus and calcium; no caffeine (nervousness); doesn't cause upset stomachs or allergic reactions. Chocolate tastes better. Two billion pounds of chocolate eaten annually in U.S. Much less carob consumed.

<u>Outline of Chocolate vs. Carob</u>

_____

_____

_____

_____

_____

_____

_____

<u>Comparison/Contrast Paper on Chocolate vs. Carob</u>

_____

_____

_____

Section 6
McDonald's vs. Arby's

Most Americans frequently eat what is called "fast food." Which fast-food restaurant is better, McDonald's or Arby's? Here is one person's opinion. Note: Since this paper was written, Arby's has stopped serving cheeseburgers and has improved its roast beef sandwiches. After completing this paper, you may see why.

Exercises

Exercise 1 (approximately 5 minutes). The following sentences describe similarities between McDonald's and Arby's. Number the sentences to form the best logical order.

___ Because the menus are limited, the food comes quickly.

168 *Comparing and Contrasting*

___ They offer a few additional food items, but basically they both have limited menus rather than the variety of foods available in regular restaurants.

___ Finally, casual dress and children are welcome at both fast-food chains.

___ McDonald's and Arby's are fast-food chains with locations throughout the country.

___ Moreover, the limited menus combined with the absence of table service result in reasonable prices.

___ Both chains offer popular fast foods: burgers, fries, and milkshakes.

Exercise 2 (approximately 10 minutes). The following sentences describe differences between McDonald's and Arby's. Categorize each sentence; write G, B, F, Sh, O, or Sum in this way:

- G- <u>general</u> statement contrasting McDonald's with Arby's on portion size and tastiness.

- B- five sentences dealing with <u>burgers</u>.

- F- two sentences dealing with <u>fries</u>.

- Sh- two sentences dealing with <u>shakes</u>.

- O- three sentences dealing with <u>other</u> items on the menu.

- Sum- <u>summary</u> sentence.

___ For example, McDonald's Big Mac, weighing 7 ounces, has cheese, sauce, lettuce, pickles, onion, and a sesame-seed bun.

___ McDonald's fries, 3 ounces, are crispy and delicious.

___ Moreover, the Big Mac's meat is tender and has a hearty beef flavor.

___ McDonald's items tend to be a little more expensive than Arby's, but the portions are larger and the food is tastier.

___ By contrast, Arby's cheeseburger, 5½ ounces, is plain and unappealing.

___ Arby's fries, 2½ ounces, are also crispy, but they are a little greasier and have a frozen potato taste somewhat like cardboard.

___ The bun is bland, lacking crispiness or flavor.
(*Vocabulary Tip: bland– dull, plain.*)

___ McDonald's chocolate shake has a rich cocoa flavor.

___ The meat has a strong, gamey flavor and a gristly texture and the cheese tastes heavily processed rather than natural.

___ In summary, the small additional cost of eating at McDonald's seems a worthwhile investment in gustatory pleasure.
(*Vocabulary Tip: gustatory– related to the sense of taste.*)

___ Turning to other items on the menu, McDonald's sells Chicken McNuggets (small pieces of batter-fried chicken) as well as fish sandwiches.

___ Arby's special feature is a roast beef sandwich consisting of a plain bun; dry, gray meat; and no sauce or gravy.

___ By contrast, Arby's chocolate shake has a weak, artificial flavor and leaves a chalky coating in the mouth.

___ The McNuggets and the sandwiches are highly palatable and have flavorful sauces.
(*Vocabulary Tip: palatable– tasty, pleasing to the palate.*)

Exercise 3 (approximately 15 minutes). Write a two-paragraph comparison/contrast paper on McDonald's and Arby's. For the first paragraph, use the sentences you numbered in Exercise 1. For the second paragraph, begin with the sentence you labeled G, next write the sentences you labeled B in the best logical order, then those labeled F, Sh, O, and Sum.

_____

_____

_____

_____

_____

_____

_____

_____

_____

_____

Exercise 4 (approximately 25 minutes). Write a comparison/contrast paper in the Block-by-Block format for any two fast-food restaurants. Note that conditions have changed in one of the restaurants just described. You may have a totally different opinion than that expressed here. You could even write a comparison/contrast paper based on the old Arby's described above and an Arby's you visit.

Section 7
Film or Print?

Which do you prefer, a good book or a fine movie? Here are some of the major similarities and differences between books and movies.

Exercises

Exercise 1 (approximately 15 minutes). Number the sentences within each paragraph to form the best logical order.

First Paragraph

___ Others insist that when a movie is made from a fine book, the movie is never as good as the original.

___ Reviewing the similarities and differences between books and movies can help a person be a better judge of this controversy, which began almost as soon as the first book was adapted for film.

___ Some people say that going to see a movie is better than curling up and reading a book.

Second Paragraph

___ Within that message they both create vicarious experiences in which you can become totally immersed.
(*Vocabulary Tips: vicarious– experienced through someone else's activities; immersed– covered and surrounded, giving something your total attention.*)

___ Both begin with the basic purpose of transferring a lasting message to a distant audience.

___ Books and movies share important qualities.

___ You live the lives, experience the situations, and feel the emotions of the main characters, who may be spies, great artists, aging sports heroes, murderers, royalty, or common people dealing with everyday problems.

Third Paragraph

___ They can take you back to the crowded streets of Rome, put you into the cockpit of a jet fighter plane, or move you forward 50 years when the earth is recovering from a nuclear war.

___ They can make you look at society, at other people, and at yourself.

_5_ The ability to create these scenarios and arouse emotions is the greatest similarity between movies and books.

___ Both books and movies provide you with avenues into the past, present, and future.

___ Sometimes the view is pleasant and tender, as in peaceful or romantic scenes; sometimes it is not, as in stories of crime, war, and poverty.

Fourth Paragraph

___ The most basic difference is that participation in these two media demands the use of different mental processes.

___ In spite of the similarities between books and movies, there are major differences between them.

___ Reading a book depends on skills developed over a long period of training and experience.

_4_ Using and enjoying books requires the ability to read well enough to create mental images of the characters, visual settings, and sounds.

_6_ The magic of cinematography produced stunning scenes like the computer-generated dinosaurs in *Jurassic Park* and the beautiful scenery translated from book to screen in *The Secret Garden*.
(Vocabulary Tip: cinematography– movie making.)

____ Movies, on the other hand, provide ready-made pictures for your eyes and sounds for your ears.

____ Movies bring all of this to people, even if they cannot read and create detailed mental images from print.

____ The voices of Marlon Brando's whispery-gruff Godfather (*The Godfather*), Clark Gable's sensuous Rhett Butler (*Gone with the Wind*), and Judy Garland's melodious Dorothy (*The Wizard of Oz*) have been enjoyed by young and old alike.

Fifth Paragraph

____ Nor did the Disney animated film *Bambi* express the plight of animals in the forest as intensely as did the German author in his original, bulky volume.

_2_ Books usually offer a more in-depth view of people's thoughts and feelings, whereas movies often limit themselves to outward actions.

____ Another difference between these media is the depth in development of the story and characters.

_4_ The sheer horror felt by the victims in the Stephen King book *Christine* was not conveyed in its film counterpart.

____ For instance, the film version of *Gone with the Wind* omits the emotional pain shared by Scarlett and Rhett at the death of their daughter.

Sixth Paragraph

____ However, to see a film you must often be in a certain place at a certain time.

_2_ Books are portable and can be used at your convenience, in the setting of your choice.
(Vocabulary Tip: portable– moveable.)

____ The physical requirements of reading a book and viewing a movie are also very different.

____ As a moviegoer, you must rely on your memory of the experience or be willing to wait and pay to see the film again.

<u> 5 </u>   Moreover, books give you the freedom to savor your favorite parts over and over again whenever and wherever you wish.

____   You must be ready to experience the entire presentation in a theater where the environment may be unpleasant because of the noise, temperature, or smells.

Seventh Paragraph

____   Both have their own merits and offer experiences that can enrich our lives.

____   Nevertheless, books are irreplaceable as my favorite media because I can enjoy them at my own convenience, and they usually provide a deeper understanding of people and situations.

____   In summary, I cannot say that all books are better than all movies, or vice versa.

Exercise 2 (approximately 15 minutes). Write the sentences in the order you numbered them to form a comparison/contrast paper for books versus movies.

_____

_____

_____

_____

_____

_____

_____

_____

_____

_____

_____

_____

_____

Exercise 3 (approximately 30 minutes). Make a chart (like that for Section 3) contrasting books and movies. You can use information from the preceding paper or from your own experiences. Then put all other material away and write a short paper contrasting books with movies. Conclude by stating which you prefer and why.

Books	Movies
_____	_____
_____	_____
_____	_____
_____	_____
_____	_____
_____	_____
_____	_____
_____	_____
_____	_____
_____	_____
_____	_____
_____	_____
_____	_____
_____	_____
_____	_____

Section 8
Analysis of Comparison/Contrast Papers

Many essay exams and papers assigned in school require comparison and contrast. In a sociology class you might compare and contrast the political attitudes of American white collar workers with those of blue collar workers. In history you might be asked to contrast Spanish with English colonization of the New World. In political science you might compare Russia's government with America's. Sometimes teachers in subjects other than English use the terms *compare* and *contrast* loosely: they may ask you to compare two things when they really mean compare and contrast.

Once you are sure of the assignment, the first step is to make a chart listing the similarities and/or differences for the two things. Such a chart was shown for Superman versus James Bond in the introduction, and for dogs versus cats in Section 3. Starting with a chart helps bring ideas to mind and organizes the ideas to form the basis for an effective paper. If you find you have listed more points in the table than you want to write about, select just those that you or your audience (e.g., teacher, employer, magazine subscribers) consider most important.

Your next step is deciding whether to employ the point-by-point or block-by-block pattern. For lengthier, more complicated topics the point-by-point pattern is easier to use. It allows you to deal with each point separately.

When you use the block-by-block pattern, you write about one thing completely and then the other. But as you write about the second thing, you must constantly refer back to the first one so your reader will think of both things together. For example, in the block by-block paper on dogs versus cats, one sentence in the middle of the second block (cats) brought dogs back to mind by beginning, "As opposed to the silly antics and noisiness of dogs, a cat is . . ."

Another way of tying the two blocks together is by using parallel structure, discussing the points in the same order within each block. In the dogs versus cats block-by-block paper the dog was first described in terms of personal needs, then noise, and finally companionship. In the second block, the cat was described on the same points in exactly the same order, so the differences between the two pets would be easy to see. If you don't use such techniques to unite the two blocks, it may seem like you are writing two separate essays.

Whichever pattern you select, certain words and phrases alert your reader to when you are discussing similarities, whereas others signal differences. Notice how "by contrast" and "but" are used in these examples to signal contrast.

> A dog is always eager to please its master and will learn new tricks like "roll over" and "get the paper." BY CONTRAST, if you try to teach the same tricks to a cat, it becomes very impatient and sneaks away as soon as possible.

> When you scold a dog, it hangs its head and with sad eyes begs for forgiveness. BUT if you scold a cat, it decides you aren't pleasant company and leaves until you change your attitude.

Here are some commonly used words and phrases for introducing comparisons and contrasts.

- Comparison (similarities)

both	<u>Both</u> movies and books . . .
similar to	Books are <u>similar to</u> movies . . .
also	Dogs <u>also</u> require . . .
like	<u>Like</u> dogs, cats must . . .
as well as	Dogs <u>as well as</u> cats offer . . .
resembles	Carob <u>resembles</u> chocolate in . . .
in common with	<u>In common with</u> movies, books provide . . .

others: *just as, in the same way, in like manner, similarly, likewise, as with*

- Contrast (differences)

unlike	<u>Unlike</u> dogs, cats are . . .
another difference between	<u>Another difference between</u> European and Japanese cars . . .
in contrast to	<u>In contrast to</u> the fuel economy of small cars . . .
whereas	<u>Whereas</u> a dog . . .
in comparison to	<u>In comparison to</u> Shakespeare's comedies, those of Mel Brooks . . .
while	<u>While</u> books require reading skill, movies . . .

others: *as opposed to, are different than, although, differ from, are dissimilar, however, but, larger than (faster than, etc.)*

To begin a comparison/contrast paper you may introduce the topic by presenting a little background information and arousing the reader's interest. However, when you are pressed for time, as with essay exams, you may start simply by describing one of the similarities or differences for the two things you are writing about.

To close the paper, you could just finish with the final comparison or contrast. But often you will write a separate sentence or paragraph to summarize the ideas you have presented. Furthermore, if you prefer one thing or feel it is better than the other, you might express this opinion in your conclusion. Of course, the opinion you express should be supported and illustrated by the remainder of the paper. Examples of papers that end with an opinion are the McDonald's versus Arby's and the books versus movies selections.

In writing the main body of a comparison/contrast paper, remember to draw upon the writing skills and techniques you developed in earlier chapters. Most important, don't just make general statements; support and illustrate them by describing specific details. For example, in contrasting cars with motorcycles, don't just say cars are more comfortable. Describe the comforts: A car is enclosed so you are sheltered from rain and wind. It has a heater to keep you warm in the winter and an air conditioner for the summer. Supporting your ideas with details is just as important in a comparison/contrast paper as in a generalization-specifics paper.

Finally, the basic comparison/contrast paper can take many forms. For instance, in making a choice between two things—two typewriters or two restaurants—the differences between them often are more important than the similarities. A paper written for such a situation might have just one paragraph on similarities and then several paragraphs describing differences. Moreover, in a point-by-point paper, you don't always have to use exactly one paragraph for each point. If two points are closely related, you might deal with them both in a single paragraph. Or if a point is important and lengthy, you might use two or more paragraphs to explain and illustrate it fully. You can adapt the comparison/contrast pattern to fit the topic and purpose of the paper you are writing.

Section 9
Independent Writing

Exercises

Exercise 1 (approximately 20 minutes). Write a paper comparing and contrasting two of your friends. You may begin by creating a chart like the one for James Bond and Superman. Your chart should compare/contrast the physical characteristics as well as the personal qualities that make each a friend. Decide before you write if you want to use the point-by-point or block-by-block format. Also make sure that your characteristics are balanced (if you write about the athletic ability of one friend, write about the athletic ability of the other friend). You may want to change the names to protect the innocent!

_____

_____

_____

_____

_____

_____

Exercise 2 (approximately 40 minutes). Write a paper (minimum 250 words) comparing and contrasting two cities (or a city vs. a town) which you have lived in, visited, or would like to see. Begin by making a table of similarities and differences. If you have trouble getting started, make a list of all the places you have been in the last year or the last ten years. Then brainstorm and write down everything you remember doing or experiencing in these places.

Exercise 3 (approximately 40 minutes). Write a paper (minimum 250 words) on one of the following topics. Begin with a table listing similarities and differences.

- Compare and contrast a car with a house trailer (RV) as methods for traveling from New York to Los Angeles.

OR

- Compare and contrast a plane with a train as methods for traveling from New York to Los Angeles.

_____

_____

_____

_____

_____

_____

_____

_____

_____

_____

_____

_____

_____

_____

_____

_____

Chapter 10
Defining

To communicate precisely, you sometimes need to define a word or term. The simplest type of definition is a synonym (a word having a similar meaning). For example, you could define the word "bizarre" by saying it means roughly the same as "strange." In defining a word this way, remember to use a synonym that is more familiar to your reader than the word you are defining. If a reader does not know what a "tumor" is, it probably will not help to write that a tumor is a "neoplasm."

Sometimes you cannot define a word with just a synonym because none exists. For instance, the word "synonym" does not have a synonym. To define "synonym" you must use a phrase like "a word having a similar meaning to another word." The word "carburetor" is another example. It has no synonym, but it can be defined by describing it with a sentence (sentence definition) such as this: A carburetor is a device on a gasoline engine used to blend and vaporize fuel and air.

Technical terms or words having personal significance (e.g., love, friendship) may require one or more paragraphs to fully explain their meaning. This is called an extended definition. For example, acid rain is mentioned in the news often. But what exactly is acid rain? An extended definition of this somewhat technical term might describe its chemical make-up, its origin, and its effect on the environment.

Turning from technical terms to personal ones with psychological impact, what do you mean by friendship? An extended definition of friendship might say friendship exists when people have common interests, show a willingness to help each other, and feel relaxed in each other's company. Each of these three expressions of friendship could be explained (and illustrated with examples) in separate paragraphs. The entire extended definition would form a paper of three or more paragraphs. The exercises in this unit illustrate extended definition papers.

Section 1
Football Fanatic

If you describe someone as a "safe driver" or a "football fanatic," you might explain what you mean by presenting several examples to illustrate the person's safe driving or football fanaticism. This is shown in the following exercises.

Exercises

Exercise 1 (approximately 5 minutes). Number the following sentences to form a paragraph describing a football fanatic.

___ He stares at football on the tube whether college or professional teams are playing.

___ He doesn't care whether it's the American, National, or Canadian league.

___ He is a TV football fanatic.
(*Vocabulary Tip: fanatic–* person who is overly enthusiastic about something.)

___ My dad isn't a football fan.

___ He spends all Saturday afternoon, Sunday afternoon, Monday and Tuesday evenings, and New Year's Day glued to the gridiron screen.
(*Vocabulary Tip: gridiron–* football field)

___ He is certainly never moved by the pleadings of other family members for conversation, household help, or a change in TV programs.
(*Vocabulary Tip: pleading–* earnest request, begging.)

___ Sometimes the rest of us wish football had never been invented.

___ An occasional trip to the kitchen or bathroom is all that moves him.

Exercise 2 (approximately 10 minutes). Write the sentences in the order you numbered them to form a paper about a TV football fanatic.

_____

_____

_____

Exercise 3 (approximately 25 minutes). Write a paper about another type of fanatic—music, studying, food, exercise, etc. Include details and, if possible, write about a person you know. For instance, if you write that your sister is a food fanatic, tell what she eats, when, how much, what food she dreams about, etc.

Section 2
Unwelcome Rain

What exactly is acid rain? The following sentences can be arranged into two paragraphs that define acid rain in terms of its composition, origin, and effects.

Exercises

Exercise 1 (approximately 10 minutes). For the first paragraph, number the sentences in the best logical order. For the second paragraph, order the destructive effects of acid rain from least to most important in your judgment. Conclude with a sentence about the future.

First Paragraph

___ These gases rise into the air, are chemically changed by sunlight, and mix with the moisture in clouds to form sulfuric and nitric acids.

___ Factories, refineries, and power plants, especially those burning high-sulfur coal, give out smoke that is thick with sulfur dioxide gas.

___ The clouds may travel hundreds of miles from the original source of pollution, but wherever they produce rain, acid is sprayed down from the sky.

___ Its main cause is air pollution.

___ Acid rain, a major environmental problem, is rain containing sulfuric and nitric acids.

___ Automobile exhaust fumes are the primary source of another pollutant, nitrogen gas. (*Vocabulary Tip: pollutant–* a substance that dirties or toxifies its environment.)

Second Paragraph

___ In humans it damages the liver, lungs, and nervous system and also causes cancer.

___ It eats away marble statues and stone buildings and destroys forests and farm crops.

___ If the human race is to remain alive and healthy into the 21st century, the causes of acid rain must be eliminated so that pure rain will again fall onto the earth.

___ Acid rain is highly destructive.

___ It kills entire populations of fish in lakes and rivers, causing million-dollar losses to fishing and tourist industries as well as threatening the existence of some fish species.

Exercise 2 (approximately 15 minutes). Write the sentences in the order you numbered them to form a two-paragraph extended definition of acid rain.

_____

_____

_____

_____

_____

_____

_____

_____

_____

Exercise 3 (approximately 20 minutes). Write two paragraphs about another source of pollution, describing the causes and effects.

Section 3
Physical Fitness

Are you really physically fit? Find out by doing the following "exercises."

Exercises

Exercise 1 (approximately 10 minutes). Number the sentences in each paragraph to form the best logical order.

First Paragraph

___ Experts say there are three components to physical fitness: cardiovascular fitness, muscular strength and endurance, and flexibility.

___ Does playing baseball on weekends or going dancing several nights a week guarantee that you are physically fit?

___ What is physical fitness?

Second Paragraph

___ You will need a sturdy box or step that is 12 inches high.

___ This component of fitness is important for living a healthy, long life.

___ Cardiovascular fitness refers to the ability of the heart, lungs, and blood vessels to deliver blood and oxygen throughout the body.

___ You can assess your cardiovascular fitness with a simple procedure called the Step Test.

___ Now step down with your right foot and then your left foot.

___ Step up with your right foot, then bring up your left foot.

___ In fact, a well-conditioned college athlete generally has a Step Test pulse of less than 85.

___ Go through this cycle 24 times a minute for 3 minutes.

___ One final word of caution: If you have a heart condition, consult your physician before taking the Step Test.

____ If your pulse rate is greater than 105 beats per minute, you could probably benefit from some cardiovascular conditioning exercise such as jogging, swimming, or cycling.

____ Then wait five seconds and take your pulse for one minute.

Third Paragraph

____ Your muscular strength differs from one body part to another, but abdominal strength is very important because these muscles help hold your internal organs in place and protect them from injury.

____ This refers to the ability of the muscles in your legs, arms, chest, and abdominal (stomach) area to exert force for a period of time.

____ To test your abdominal strength, see how many bent-leg sit-ups you can do.

____ The second component of fitness is muscular strength and endurance.

____ Never perform straight-leg sit-ups because they can injure your back.

____ Roll up (don't jerk) until your elbows touch your knees, then return to the starting position.

____ If you can't do 30 sit-ups, practice them about five days per week until your abdominal muscles meet this mark.

____ Lie down with your legs bent to form a right angle at the knees and place your hands behind your head.

Fourth Paragraph

____ For example, if you lack lower back flexibility, you are more likely to hurt your back bending over to lift something.

____ Slowly reach forward as far as you can.

____ To test your lower back flexibility, sit on the floor with your legs together and straight.

____ The final component of fitness, flexibility, concerns your ability to bend and stretch parts of your body fully.

____ If you can't, you might consider starting a program of stretching exercises to increase your flexibility.

____ Flexibility is important in avoiding muscle and joint injuries.

____ Consider yourself flexible if you can reach five inches beyond your toes.

Fifth Paragraph

___ However, a sports physician or physical education instructor can provide a more thorough evaluation of your overall fitness and can recommend an exercise program to improve and maintain your fitness for life.

___ The tests just described illustrate the three components of fitness.

Exercise 2 (approximately 15 minutes). Write the sentences in the order you numbered them to form an extended definition of physical fitness.

Exercise 3 (approximately 30 minutes). Based on the previous exercise or your own experience, make a paragraph-by-paragraph outline of facts for an extended definition paper on physical fitness. Limit your outline to a total of 100 words. Then put all other material away and write the paper (minimum 300 words) from the outline. Remember to read your first draft critically, correct spelling or grammar errors, and revise any sentences that can be rewritten to sound better or express ideas more clearly.

Physical Fitness Outline

_____
_____
_____
_____
_____
_____
_____
_____
_____
_____
_____

Physical Fitness Paper

_____
_____
_____
_____
_____
_____

Section 4
Stepparent Blues

What associations does the word "stepparent" bring to mind? Do you think of a mean, selfish person like Cinderella's stepmother? Here is the meaning of "stepparent" for a writer who is a stepparent.

Exercises

Exercise 1 (approximately 15 minutes). Number the sentences within each paragraph to form the best logical order.

First Paragraph

____ It simply describes a stepparent as "the person who has married one's parent after the death or divorce of the other parent."

____ A Webster's dictionary gives a rather superficial definition of the word "stepparent."
(*Vocabulary Tip: superficial– surface, shallow, not deep.*)

____ However, most stepparents have had experiences that give a much broader meaning to the word.

____ This definition makes it seem easy to be a stepparent.

Second Paragraph

____ But the word still sounds ugly and carries mean connotations.
(*Vocabulary Tip: connotations– associations suggested by a word.*)

____ Today, as the divorce rate soars, the stepparent is becoming a common member of the family unit.

__3__ For centuries, stepparents have received more than their fair share of unkind press.

____ In fact, due to these and other stories, stepmothers have become so suspect that many tales made up by children contain a "wicked stepmother" who terrorizes everyone in the fantasy.
(*Vocabulary Tip: suspect– open to suspicion.*)

____ After all, wasn't it Cinderella's stepmother who almost worked the poor child to death?

198 *Defining*

___ And wasn't Snow White's stepmother so jealous that she tried to kill the little princess?

_7_ Stepfathers haven't fared much better.

___ Also, Mr. Murdstone in *David Copperfield* proved to be about as cruel as a stepfather could be.

___ And tabloids have spread the news of stepfathers who have abused, molested, and murdered their stepchildren.
(*Vocabulary Tip: tabloid– newspaper with sensationalistic news and gossip.*)

___ In *Hamlet*, it was the stepfather who tried to murder the Danish prince.

Third Paragraph

___ Now, I hear protests of, "You don't know my stepmother (or stepfather)!" from some of you, and I admit you are right.

___ Although in reality some stepparents are wicked and abusive, many more are good and kind to their stepchildren.

___ But if the majority of you are honest, you will have to admit that your stepparent really isn't an ogre waiting for the chance to ruin your life forever.
(*Vocabulary Tip: ogre– monster.*)

___ I don't know your stepparent, and he or she may be terrible.

Fourth Paragraph

___ And through the games of ego versus ego versus id, I have learned well the roles I am expected to play.
(*Vocabulary Tips: ego– self-pride, self-esteem; id– primary instincts.*)

___ The experiences that I've had are like a mixture of homemade sweet and sour sauce; even now I never know just what the "taste" of any situation is going to be.

___ Putting all the fantastic tales and dictionary definitions aside, I believe I know what a stepparent really is because for five years I've known the burdens and the joys that accompany the title.

Fifth Paragraph

___ I have also learned how to act at my husband's family gatherings when the other grandparents drop in and stay for hours reminiscing about the happy times when "the children" were married.
(*Vocabulary Tip: reminiscing– thinking or talking about the past.*)

___ As a stepparent I have learned to play the role of the cause for the breakup of my husband's first marriage and the disruptive effects it had on my stepchild, even though the marriage ended long before my husband and I met.

Sixth Paragraph

___ And early in my marriage I learned how to play the one who stayed at home when an outing suddenly became a "twosome."

_2_ Then I was expected to be the "absentee" when they could be present.

___ Another role I learned was that of the "attendee" (my word) at school plays, dance recitals, and music extravaganzas when the real parents couldn't be there.

___ But the most hurtful part I learned to play was how to watch my stepchild give good-night kisses to everyone in the room—except me.

Seventh Paragraph

___ And more than once I have been a protector when tasks went undone or standards were not met.

_2_ Also, I have been the advocate when whiney whims became angry demands that soon turned to pitiful cries.
(*Vocabulary Tips: advocate– a person who argues for the welfare of another; whims– sudden wishes or desires.*)

___ Some of the sweeter times have occurred when my role required me to become a co-conspirator in helping acquire some wanted treasure, such as roller skates, a bicycle, or a computer.
(*Vocabulary Tips: co-conspirator– one who aids in a plan; acquire– to obtain.*)

___ But these feelings lasted only until it was time for the child to visit the other parent, and he rushed off without remembering to say good-bye.

___ During those times I said to myself, "I am the only person in the world who really understands this child."

Eighth Paragraph

___ Who knows, maybe I'll even be invited to the wedding.

___ Sometimes I think I do it just to find out if the good times will ever catch up with the bad ones.

___ It is not easy to ride the emotional seesaw of stepparenthood day after day.

Exercise 2 (approximately 15 minutes). Write the sentences in the order you numbered them to form an extended definition paper for "stepparent."

Section 5
Analysis of Extended Definition Papers

This unit has been placed last in the text because writing an extended definition generally taps the variety of the writing skills covered in previous chapters. In writing extended definitions for "football fanatic," "acid rain," "physical fitness," and "stepparent," people and situations were described, cause-effect relationships were explained, sequences of actions were recounted, and examples were presented to illustrate general ideas. In this sense, writing extended definitions draws on all the writing skills practiced earlier.

The Stepparent Blues paper highlighted an important distinction made regarding words that have personal or emotional meaning. The paper distinguished between the *denotative* meaning of "stepparent" and the *connotative* meaning to the writer. The denotative meaning of a word is the definition that you find in the dictionary; it is basically the same for everyone. "Stepparent," for instance, has the following denotative meaning: the person who has married one's parent after the death or divorce of the other parent.

The connotative meaning of a word includes the feelings it suggests. For example, a person's "home" is more than just a building for shelter from the weather. "Home" has associated feelings that can produce "homesickness" when you are away from "home sweet home." These feelings form the connotative meaning of "home." The connotative meaning of a word is not the same for everyone because people's experiences differ. The Stepparent Blues paper presented the connotative meaning of "stepparent" for the writer, herself a stepparent. A connotative meaning paper allows a writer to communicate personal feelings, helping people understand each other and themselves better. A stepchild (or the spouse of a stepparent) might develop greater sensitivity in family situations after reading the Stepparent Blues paper. And another stepparent with similar frustrations could obtain comfort from reading the paper and realizing that he or she is not alone with these experiences. If an extended definition paper that you write brings greater insight and sensitivity to others, you have achieved a primary goal of writing.

Section 6
Independent Writing

Exercise

Exercise (approximately 45 minutes). Write an extended definition of some term that is meaningful to you (for example, teenager, friendship, growing up). Contrast the denotative and connotative definitions of the term to help the reader understand your perspective, as was done in Stepparent Blues.

Next Steps: Analyze, Organize, and Write on Your Own

The chapters you have just completed illustrate some major patterns of thinking and writing. But you probably noticed that the pattern presented in each chapter was frequently used in the papers of other chapters as well. For example, the cheese classification paper (Chapter 5) and the McDonald's vs. Arby's comparison/contrast paper (Chapter 9) both included descriptions of how things looked and tasted (Chapter 1). The cheese paper described the cheese-making process and the steel drums paper described drum tuning, although process papers are the focus of Chapter 3. And the wheat kernel paper of Chapter 1 drew a comparison to an egg as a visual aid. In fact, classification papers almost always include statements on comparisons of objects in different categories, while comparison/contrast papers generally classify characteristics as "similar" and "different," and then further classify them into categories like—in dogs versus cats—personal needs, noise, and companionship.

In your own writing, combine the patterns in the ways that allow you to best communicate your ideas. In a paper about commercial passenger planes you might begin with a physical description of a typical jet airliner; then recount the history of passenger planes; next describe some activities and operations—such as boarding, taking off, and eating; and finally present some statistics and examples showing the importance of passenger planes in today's world. Several of the extended definition papers show other examples of how patterns can be combined. For instance, the Physical Fitness paper has the overall organization of a classification paper (three categories of fitness), but within each category there is a short instructions paper explaining how you can evaluate yourself on that component of fitness.

The patterned exercises in this book have strengthened your abilities to analyze relations and express ideas in standard written English. But as the above examples show, writing patterns can be combined in different ways to fit different topics. The only general pattern or approach to use in writing almost any paper is to state your main points clearly, support and illustrate them with concrete examples and descriptions, and be willing to rewrite your paper several times as, each time you reread the paper, you think of more effective ways to communicate your thoughts.